RUGBY UNION
▾ LAWS ▾
Illustrated

RUGBY UNION
▾ LAWS ▾
Illustrated

CLIVE NORLING with TERRY GODWIN

PELHAM BOOKS

First published in Great Britain by
Pelham Books Ltd
44 Bedford Square
London WC1B 3DP
1985

British Library Cataloguing in Publication Data

Norling, Clive
  Rugby laws illustrated.
  1. Rugby football—Rules
  I. Title II. Godwin, Terry
  796.33′3′02022   GV945.4

  ISBN 0 7207 1622 5

Printed in Great Britain by
Butler & Tanner Ltd, Frome and London

CONTENTS

PART II

LAWS OF THE GAME OF RUGBY FOOTBALL

FOREWORD

By HERMAS EVANS

The Laws of the Game of Rugby Football were very brief when William Webb Ellis, with a fine disregard for the rules of football as played at that time, first took the ball in his arms and ran with it. As the game expanded the Laws became more extensive in depth and number, and today, it is truly a formidable task to study and digest them. The International Rugby Football Board, the body responsible for the promulgation of the Laws of the Game, has periodically found it necessary to introduce changes in the Laws which have maintained the growing popularity of the game. In framing the Laws, whereby all the principles of the game have been retained, the Board has always tried to give every opportunity for imaginative play and every advantage to the team willing to attack, to vary its game, and to keep it going. Nevertheless, despite these worthy efforts, there is a general complaint that the Laws are still too complicated to follow with ease and understanding, especially to players, coaches and spectators.

The Board has from time to time issued rulings to explain a Law; it has undertaken major reviews; and in 1976 it instigated a re-write of the Laws with a view to their simplification and improvement in clarity. The latter was an abortive attempt and one of personal disappointment – I feel that the exercise will have to be resurrected in the near future for the good and safety of the game. The present situation is far from satisfactory and in addition it is responsible for too frequent changes in the Laws, a situation that no one likes.

Many rugby enthusiasts and organisations have produced some very useful guidelines and comments on the Laws of Rugby Football; others have written on the skills, and art of refereeing; some have commented on the application of the Laws in coaching manuals and books; and one has to praise the very good wall charts to illustrate aspects of the game and the related Laws. It is therefore with a feeling of great interest to find that Clive Norling has decided to attach his name, experience, versatility, and quite often imagination to this illustrated survey of the Laws, supplemented with hints to players, referees and coaches. It is not a survey on how the game should be played, but on the important and related aspect of making the correct and best use of the Laws for enjoying the game. His term of reference is the existing Laws and he has explained the main points of each with accompanying illustrations and diagrams. I have always regretted the decision to remove diagrams from the official Laws of the Game as they can help in making the intentions more clear. He has refrained from mentioning obtrusive points of Law as they could only confuse the issue.

Clive has proved himself as one of the game's outstanding referees with an inimitable style and approach, greatly respected and favoured by the players. He is no stranger to controversy but he has admirable courage and conviction to deal with same. He tolerates no indiscipline and has a tactful but firm approach in dealing with all possible awkward situations that frequently arise on the field of play. Clive thinks avidly of the game, and how it should be best played and controlled for enjoyment and safety. His vast knowledge and experience is now in print and I feel certain that this book will be invaluable to all concerned with the game of Rugby Football. There is certainly a demand for a book of this description, and one hopes that it will be continually updated.

Finally, whatever is spoken and written on the Laws of the Game, the enjoyment of playing Rugby Football must still in the long run depend on the attitude of players in maintaining fitness and on their understanding of the intention of introducing rules and discipline into the game. It is best summed up in the following extract from 'The Object of the Game':

> 'observing fair play according to the Laws and a sporting spirit'.

HERMAS EVANS

Life Member & Trustee of the W.R.U.
Former President W.R.U. (1982–83)
W.R.U. Representative on International Board (1969–82)
Former Chairman of International Board 1977
Former Chairman of the International Board Laws Committee and Re-write of the Laws Committee

ACKNOWLEDGEMENTS

The authors and publishers are grateful to the International Rugby Football Board for permission to reproduce the official Laws of the Game.

Illustrations: by Graham Howells, of the Dyfed College of Art, Carmarthen.

INTRODUCTION

It has been said that Rugby Football is a simple game: only the Laws are complex. The reverse of that could be argued, for over the years the law-makers have striven – not always successfully – to avoid ambiguity so that the game can be played and understood by players at all levels. However, so many diverse and perplexing events can occur during a match, that players and referees can be non-plussed and would require an encyclopaedic memory to interpret and react to all the situations.

The aim of this book is not so much to clarify the Laws, or remove ambiguity, or to challenge them in any way, but to try to simplify them and make the essentials of the game easier to understand, for player and referee, whether he be a newcomer to the game or an old hand. The book does not attempt to 'water down' the Laws, but seeks to provide guidelines for a better understanding and appreciation of them and the game itself. If enjoyment of the game should increase because of this, that is justification in itself for the book's production.

Many of the Laws, or parts of them, are clear and self-explanatory and need no interpretation. These are contained in the full list of the Laws, as framed by the International Rugby Football Board, in Part II.

In general terms, those Laws that are dealt with in Part I, the 'interpretative' section of the book, follow a straightforward formula: what a player *can* or *cannot* do in given situations. The logic of this approach assumes that if a player is made clearly aware of what he is allowed to do, he is less likely to commit a breach of the Law and risk the consequences. Hopefully, by the same token, if a player is educated as to what he cannot do, life for a referee at least will be far simpler. The Questions and Answers supplement to this formula is intended to stress points of Law, or to remove any doubts concerning situations which experience tells us are among the most common during a match.

It is also hoped that this formula indirectly underlines the spirit which should accompany the playing of the game of rugby football. No game would be worth the playing unless such an appreciation of that spirit is accepted. The law-makers have sought to ensure that all players embrace this idea, that fair play is a prerequisite and that enjoyment in participating is fundamental. This book is intended as a modest extension of those ideals.

TERRY GODWIN

The following illustrated section is a summary of the twenty-eight Laws of Rugby Football. It is by necessity a selective summary, containing the essential elements for playing the game, and using a language intentionally simple. Care has been taken not to depart fundamentally from the official wording. Each section has been treated in a logical progression rather than a strict numerical one, as in the Laws themselves. The sheer volume of the Laws makes it impossible to deal with every aspect of the game; should the reader wish for more detailed explanations and advisory notes on any specific Law he should cross-refer to the full list of Laws in Part II on pages 57–107.

GENERAL LAWS

BEFORE KICK-OFF

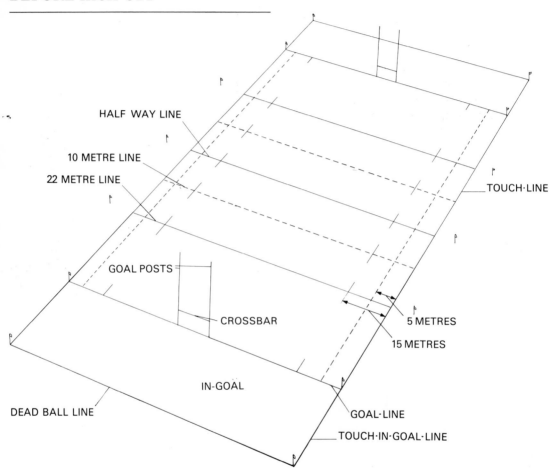

HALF WAY LINE

10 METRE LINE

22 METRE LINE

TOUCH·LINE

GOAL POSTS

CROSSBAR

5 METRES

15 METRES

IN-GOAL

DEAD BALL LINE

GOAL-LINE

TOUCH·IN·GOAL·LINE

LAW 1 The Playing Area

Rugby is played on a rectangular field, and the field is divided into equal halves.

The size of the field may be varied between given maximum limits according to the space available.

LAW 2 The Ball

Rugby is played with a ball which is oval in shape.
  Its size, weight and pressure are specified.
  The dimensions of the ball may be reduced only for younger schoolboys.

q *Can the ball be changed during a match?*
  Yes, it is normal practice to have more than one ball available. However, the ball cannot be changed for a penalty kick at goal or for a conversion. The ball which is in play must be used for kicks at goal.
  See Law 28(1). Also Notes: Law 13(8), Law 27(1).

q *Can the ball be treated to make it resistant to mud and easier to grip?*
  Yes. See Law 2(3).

LAW 3 The Player

In every match there are two teams, each having not more than fifteen players.

A player may be replaced only because of injury, and once he has been replaced he may not resume playing in that match. A maximum of two replacements are allowed in senior matches.

In matches between teams of schoolboys or teams where all players are under the age of 19, up to *six* players may be replaced.

q *A team starts a match with only fourteen players. The fifteenth player arrives ten minutes after the match has kicked off. May he join his team?*

Yes, provided the referee is advised. If the match is in progress the player must wait until the ball is dead, and the referee signals for him to come on to the field of play.

q *After a match has been in progress for some time, one of the captains points out to the referee that the other side has sixteen players on the field. Does this affect the score, and what action should the referee take?*

The objection does not affect any score previously attained, but the referee must ask the captain of the team with sixteen players to reduce the number of players appropriately.

q *Can a player who has been sent off by the referee be replaced?*

No. A replacement may only be allowed because of injury.

q *A player has had to leave the field of play for treatment of an injury. When can he return to his team?*

When there is a stoppage in play and the referee gives a signal for the player to return.

LAW 4 Players' Dress

The main point of this Law is to prevent a player wearing anything which is dangerous to another player.

The referee shall order a player to remove any dangerous projection, such as a ring, which could cause injury.

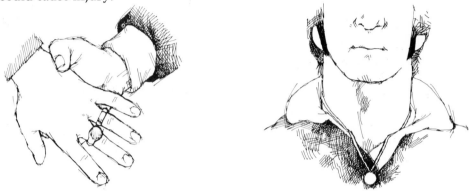

Players' boot studs must be of leather, rubber, aluminium or any approved plastic to conform to British Standard BS6366.

The wearing of a single stud at the toe of the boot is prohibited.

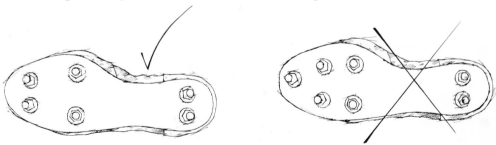

q *During a match can a referee decide that a part of a player's dress is dangerous?*

Yes. The referee has the power to decide before or during a match; he must order the player to remove the dangerous part and only allow the player to continue playing after it has been removed.

LAW 5 Toss, Time

It is normal before a match for the two captains to toss a coin for the right either:
(a) to kick off, or
(b) to make a choice of ends.

The duration of play in a match shall not exceed 80 minutes, and is made up of two equal halves of 40 minutes. These times may be reduced for younger players. Certain competitions allow for extra time to be played in the event of there being no result at the end of the normal period.

Any time lost for injury or any permitted delay shall be added on by the referee to the half in which it occurs.

q *A player is taking a place kick at goal. How long can he take before the referee starts adding on time for 'undue delay' on the part of the kicker?*

Playing time lost should start 40 seconds after the kicker has indicated his intention to kick for goal.

MODE OF PLAY

LAW 7 Mode of Play

Once a match has been started by a kick-off, any player who is on-side and *provided* he plays within the laws of the game, *can* at any time:

Catch or pick up the ball and run with it.

Pass, throw, or knock the ball *back* to another player.

Kick or otherwise propel the ball.

Tackle, push or shoulder
an opponent
holding the ball.

Fall on the ball.

A player may also take part in:

a scrummage

a ruck

a maul

a line-out

LAWS OF PLAY

SCORING VALUES

LAW 11 Method of Scoring

The methods of scoring and their scoring values are:
   A try   4 points
   A goal scored after a try (conversion)   2 points
   A goal from a penalty kick   3 points
   A dropped goal otherwise obtained   3 points

KICK-OFF AND OTHER KICKS

LAW 10 Kick-off

All kick-offs are taken from the centre of the half-way line.
   A place kick is used:
   to start the match,
   to re-start play after the half-time interval,
   after a team has scored a goal.
   A drop-kick is used:
   after an unconverted try.

The correct type of kick must always be used, the ball must reach the opposition ten metre line, and the ball must land or be touched in the field of play.

The kicker's team must be behind the ball when kicked. The opposing team must stand on or behind their ten metre line.

q *If the ball is not kicked ten metres at a kick-off what is the option open to the opposing team?*

Have the ball kicked off again, or have a scrummage formed at the centre of the half-way line. However, if the opponents advance and play the ball before it goes ten metres then play shall continue.

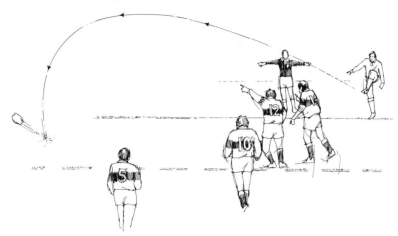

q *If, from the kick-off, the ball is kicked directly into touch, touch-in-goal or over or on the dead-ball line, what choice is open to the opposing team?*

They may accept the kick, have the ball kicked off again or have a scrummage formed at the centre of the half-way line.

LAW 13 Kick at Goal after a Try

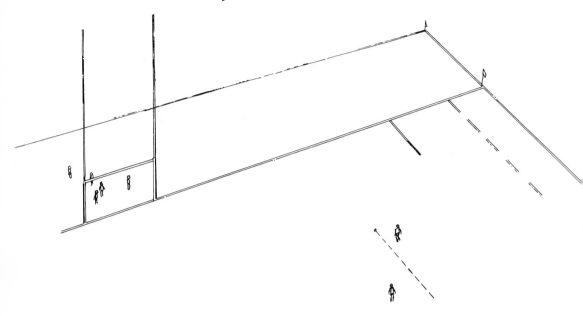

After a try has been scored, the scoring side are allowed to kick for goal. The kicker may take either a place kick or a drop-kick anywhere on a line through the place where the try was scored.

The kicker's team must be behind the ball when it is kicked. The opposing team must be behind the goal-line.

q *Can the defending team shout during a kick at goal?*

No. Should they do so, the referee shall order another kick without the charge.

q *When may opponents charge in order to prevent a goal?*

When the kicker offers to kick or when he begins his run.

LAW 15 Drop-out

A drop-out kick at the twenty-two metre line is awarded to the defending team after either:

(a) the attacking team commit an offence in-goal, or

(b) the attacking team put the ball into the in-goal area and it is made dead (touched-down) by the defending team.

To re-start the match at a drop-out:

the ball must be drop-kicked by a defender behind the twenty-two metre line,

the ball must then reach the twenty-two metre line,

the ball must land or be touched in the field of play.

q *Can an attacking player cross the twenty-two metre line to charge the ball down?*

No.

The kicker's team must be behind the ball when it is kicked. The opposing team must stand on the opposite side of the twenty-two metre line.

q *If the ball does not reach the twenty-two metre line or it pitches directly into touch, what are the options open to the attacking team?*

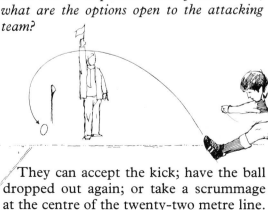

They can accept the kick; have the ball dropped out again; or take a scrummage at the centre of the twenty-two metre line.

LAW 27 Penalty Kick LAW 28 Free Kick

For a deliberate or wilful infringement of the Laws the referee will award either:

(a) a penalty kick – which allows a direct kick at goal, or

(b) a free kick – which is indirect and from which a goal cannot be *immediately* scored.

Where the referee has awarded a free kick for a fair catch, only the catcher can kick the ball. In all other cases, for a penalty kick or free kick, any player can take the kick either by a place kick, drop-kick or punt.

The kicker's team must be behind the ball when it is kicked. The opposing team must be ten metres from the original mark.

q *Must the penalty kick or free kick be taken exactly at the original mark?*

No. The kick may be taken at the original mark or on a line which is through the mark and parallel to the touch-lines.

q *Can the kicker kick the ball in any direction?*

Yes.

q *Can the opposing team charge a penalty kick or free kick?*

They cannot charge a penalty kick, but in the case of a free kick they are allowed to charge as soon as the kicker offers to kick or begins his run.

q *Can a penalty kick or free kick be taken within five metres of the opposing goal-line?*

No.

OPEN PLAY

LAW 12 Try and Touch-down

A try is scored in the opponents' in-goal area when a player:

While holding the ball in his hand or hands, brings the ball into contact with the ground.

If the ball is on the ground, places his hand or arm on it with downward pressure.

If the ball is on the ground, falls on it with the ball anywhere under the front of his body from waist to neck inclusive.

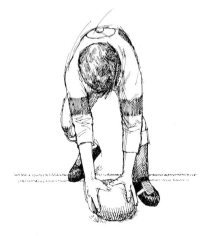

q *What is the referee's decision when an attacking player kicks the ball over his opponents' goal-line and is about to fall on the ball when he is held back by an opponent?*

A penalty try is awarded between the posts. The attacking player would *probably* have scored but for foul play by his opponent.

A touch-down is the same action as a try except that the *defending* player grounds the ball first in his *own* in-goal area.

LAW 18 Tackle

A player carrying the ball is deemed to have been tackled when he is held by an opponent and then brought to the ground while held.

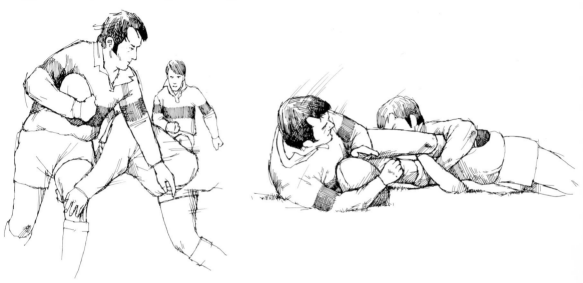

Tackled player must immediately:
release the ball,
move away from the ball.
Both tackled player and tackler must:
get back on their feet before playing the ball again.

N.B. A player can play the ball in any way, including pushing it away or passing the ball to another player *as long as the action is immediate and the ball does not go forward.*

q *If a player is knocked over but not held by an opponent, must he release the ball?*
    No. As he is not held it is not a tackle.

q *A player is tackled but his momentum takes him into the opponents' in-goal area. Can a try be awarded?*
    Yes.

LAW 16 Fair Catch (Mark)

A fair catch is a method of legally stopping play during a match.

In order to make a fair catch a player must:

be inside his own twenty-two metre area,

be stationary,

have both feet on the ground,

catch the ball cleanly direct from an opponent's kick, knock-on or throw-forward,

at the same time as the above, shout 'MARK!'

If all the above are complied with the referee will award a free kick.

q *What if the defending player is injured in making a fair catch and is unable to take the free kick?*

A scrummage shall be formed at the mark, the defending side putting in the ball.

MARK !

LAW 17 Knock-on or Throw-forward

The ball must always be passed backwards so as not to infringe the Law.

It is therefore a knock-on if the ball goes forward off a player's hand or arm towards his opponents' dead-ball line, and it is a throw-forward when a player carrying the ball throws or passes it in the direction of his opponents' dead-ball line. In each case the ball must hit another player or the ground.

q *Can a player deliberately knock the ball forward?*

No.

q *Can a player intercept an opponent's pass by knocking the ball forward?*

No.

q *Is it a knock-on if a player charges down an opponent's kick?*

No.

q *When a player attempting to catch the ball knocks it forward accidentally but catches it again before it hits the ground, is that a knock-on?*

No. In an accidental knock forward the ball must touch another player or hit the ground.

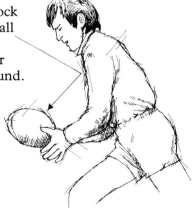

LAW 19 Lying With, On or Near the Ball

A player can fall on the ball in open play, and provided he has not been tackled, he *can*:

pass the ball to another player,

get up on to his feet with the ball,

push the ball away from him.

However a player on the ground *cannot*:
hold on to the ball,
lie on or curl around the ball,
prevent an opponent gaining possession.

Other players cannot:
wilfully fall or dive on or over a player/players on the ground with the ball in his/their possession,
fall on or over the ball emerging from a scrummage or ruck.

Players on one knee or both knees or sitting on the ground are deemed to be lying on the ground.

THE GET-TOGETHERS

LAW 21 Ruck

A ruck consists of:
 the ball on the ground in the field of play,
 at least one player from either side in physical contact standing over the ball between them.

Players must join the ruck from their own side and from behind the ball, and must bind with at least one arm around the body of a player of his team in the ruck.
 Players must stay standing on their feet in the ruck and are only allowed to play the ball with their feet.

q *Can a player handle the ball in a ruck at any time?*
 No.

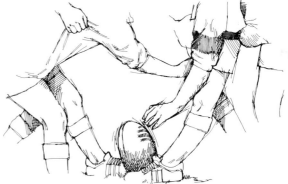

q *Can a player bind in a ruck with just his hand?*
 No. He must bind with the whole arm from hand to shoulder.

LAW 22 Maul

A maul consists of:

a player carrying the ball, and who is standing on his feet in the field of play, at least one player from *either* side is in physical contact closing around the ball carrier, standing on their feet.

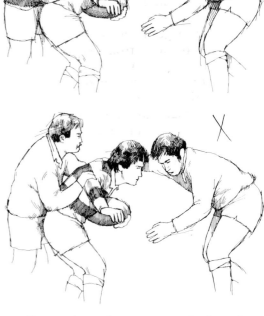

Players must join the maul from their own side, and from behind the ball.

q *Can a player deliberately pull the leg of a player in a maul in order to collapse it?*
No. That is dangerous play.

q *What is physical contact in a maul?*
A player who is caught in the middle of the maul or is bound to the maul by his arm.

q *Can a player jump on top of other players in the maul?*
No. That is dangerous play.

SET-PIECE PLAY

LAW 20 Scrummage

A scrummage is the way of re-starting play after an unintentional infringement of the Laws.

A scrummage is a set formation in which the forwards from both sides pack down in the field of play, leaving a tunnel between them into which the scrum-half puts the ball.

A scrummage can only begin when it is stationary and the tunnel is parallel to the goal-lines.

Only three players are allowed to be in the front row at any one time, although a minimum of five players per side must form the scrum.

Each player in the scrummage must:
be in a position for an effective forward shove,
stand on both feet at all times,
only play the ball with his feet,
bind with at least one arm around the body of a team-mate.

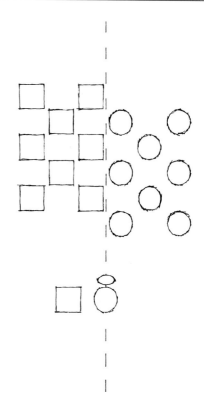

FRONT ROW BINDING
Players in the front row must bind continuously below the armpits.

Both front rows must stay bound with each other until the ball is out of the scrummage.

PROPS BINDING

A tight-head prop's right arm must be *outside* the left arm of the loose-head prop.

OTHER PLAYERS' BINDING

A player must bind with one arm around the body of another player of his own team in the scrummage.

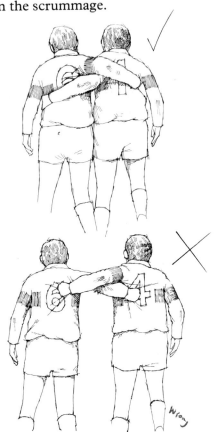

OR

A loose-head prop can place his left arm on his left thigh for support.

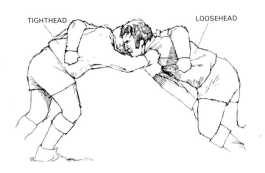

A scrum-half must:

stand one metre from the scrummage, stand midway between both front rows, hold the ball with both hands between knee and ankle, put the ball into scrum with a single forward movement at a quick speed.

38

q *Which team puts the ball into a set scrummage?*

The team *not* responsible for the infringement of Law or the stoppage of play.

q *What if the referee is unable to decide who was responsible for the stoppage? (This also applies when a maul becomes unplayable.)*

He awards the put-in to the scrummage to the team who were last going forward, or to the attacking team.

q *Is the scrummage always held where the infringement occurs?*

Yes. Except where the infringement occurs within five metres of the touch-line, when the scrummage is moved in five metres from the touch-line.

q *Can a prop forward pull his opposite number to wheel or collapse a scrum?*

No.

q *If the ball goes straight through the tunnel without being hooked can play continue?*

No. Normally the ball must be hooked for play to continue.

q *Can the scrum-half kick the ball when it is in the scrummage?*

No.

q *Can a flanker leave the scrummage when the ball is still in the scrummage?*

Yes, as long as the ball is in front of the flanker and not behind him.

LAW 23 Touch and Line-out

A line-out is the method of re-starting the match when the ball is in touch.

The ball is in touch when it touches the touch-line or the ground or a person beyond it. If the ball is being carried, it is touch if the player carrying the ball touches the touch-line or the ground beyond it.

A line-out takes place between the five and fifteen metre lines. It consists of a minimum of two players from each team who must be at least one metre from another player of their own team and 500mm from their opponents.

The ball must be thrown in, without delay, by an opponent of the player who last touched the ball, and at the place indicated.

The ball must be thrown five metres. The player throwing in must not have a foot in the field of play; he must throw in at the place indicated and the ball must land or be played anywhere along the line of touch. Only players jumping for the ball can move before the ball has been touched in the line-out. Then players must jump unassisted or unhindered.

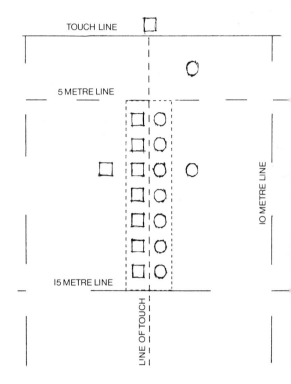

TOUCH LINE

5 METRE LINE

10 METRE LINE

15 METRE LINE

LINE OF TOUCH

Line-out begins:
when ball leaves the hand of the thrower-in.

Line-out ends:
when the ball leaves the line-out,
when the ball is thrown beyond the fifteen metre line,
when the player carrying the ball leaves the line-out,
if the line-out turns into a ruck or maul,
when all feet are clear of the line of touch,
if the ball becomes unplayable.

PEELING-OFF

Player leaves the line-out to catch the ball knocked back by a team-mate. Player peeling must run close to the line-out.

QUICK THROW-IN

This is allowed before line-out has formed, provided only players have touched the ball, and the same ball is used. All other requirements must be followed, i.e. the ball must be thrown five metres, etc.

q *Can a player lift or assist one of his team-mates to catch a ball at a line-out?*
No.

OFF-SIDE AND ON-SIDE

LAW 24 Off-side   LAW 25 On-side

In general play a player is in an off-side position if he is in front of the ball when it was last played by another player of *his* team.

At a scrummage, ruck, maul or line-out a player is off-side if he remains or advances in front of the required 'off-side' line.

On-side means that a player is in the game and can play the ball.

All players who are 'off-side' must make an effort to return on-side and must not loiter.

OFF-SIDE IN GENERAL PLAY

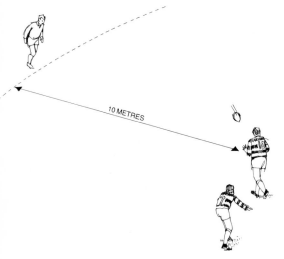

10 METRES

Any off-side player is out of the game, so in general play must not play the ball, obstruct an opponent or approach to within ten metres of where the ball pitches.

ON-SIDE IN GENERAL PLAY

A player is on-side:

(a) *By his own action* of retiring *behind* the player of his team who last played the ball.

(b) *By action of his team*, when the player of the team carrying the ball is in front of him, or when an 'on-side'

player of his team comes from behind where the ball was last played and runs past him.

(c) *By action of opponents*, when an opponent carrying the ball runs five metres or when an opponent kicks or passes the ball, or when an opponent intentionally touches the ball and does not catch or gather it.

OFF-SIDE AT SCRUMMAGE, RUCK OR MAUL

Participating players are off-side if they join from their opponents' side or join in front of the ball.

Players who are not participating must remain behind the off-side line.

Off-side players retiring at scrummage, ruck or maul become on-side when an opponent carrying the ball runs five metres or when an opponent kicks the ball.

q *Can an off-side player at a scrummage, ruck or maul be put on-side if an opponent passes the ball?*

No.

OFF-SIDE AT A LINE-OUT

The thrower-in and his opponent:

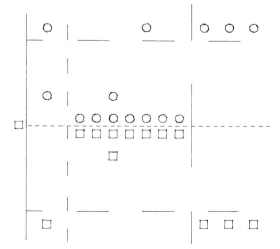

can stay within five metre line,
retire to ten metre off-side line,
can join the line-out,
if no scrum-half in position, can move to have ball knocked back to him.

All players must stay in line-out until the line-out has ended, except if 'peeling' to catch the ball.

Before ball has been touched:
a player participating in line-out is off-side if he crosses line of touch.

After ball has been touched a player:
is off-side if he goes in front of the ball,
must not leave line-out except for a 'peel',
must not move beyond fifteen metre line *except* if ball is being thrown direct to the player who moves back over the fifteen metre line.

Players not participating in line-out:
cannot advance to within ten metres of the line-out, before line-out has ended *except* when the ball is thrown directly to them.

q *A player is in front of one of his team who has just kicked the ball. The ball hits the back of an opponent. Can the original off-side player now play the ball?*

No. An opponent must intentionally touch the ball before he places an off-side player back on-side.

q *Can a player be off-side in his own in-goal area?*

Yes.

q *Can any action put on-side an off-side player standing within ten metres of an opponent wanting to play the ball?*

No. The player himself must move ten metres away from the opponent wanting to play the ball.

FOUL PLAY

LAW 26 Foul Play

Foul Play is any action by a player which is contrary to the letter and spirit of the game and includes obstruction, unfair play, misconduct, dangerous play, unsporting behaviour, retaliation and repeated infringements.

OBSTRUCTION

It is illegal for any player:

who is running for the ball to charge or push an opponent also running for the ball, except shoulder to shoulder,

who is in an off-side position wilfully to run or stand in front of another player of his team who is carrying the ball,

who is carrying the ball after it has come out of a scrummage, ruck, maul or line-out, to attempt to force his way through the players of his team in front of him,

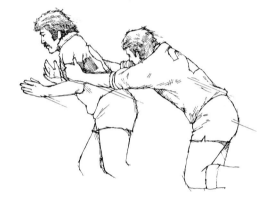

N.B. There are no circumstances in which a player carrying the ball can be penalised for obstruction.

UNFAIR PLAY AND REPEATED INFRINGEMENTS

It is illegal for any player:

deliberately to play unfairly or wilfully infringe any Law,

wilfully to waste time,

wilfully to knock or throw the ball from the playing area into touch, touch-in-goal or over the dead-ball line,

to infringe repeatedly any Law.

who is an outside player in a scrummage or ruck to prevent an opponent from advancing round the scrummage or ruck.

MISCONDUCT AND DANGEROUS PLAY
It is illegal for any player:
 to strike an opponent,

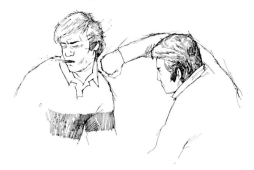

wilfully to hack or kick an opponent or to trip him with the foot or to trample on an opponent lying on the ground,

in the front row of a scrummage to form down some distance from the opponents and rush against them,
wilfully to cause a scrummage or ruck to collapse,
while the ball is out of play to molest, obstruct or in any way interfere with an opponent or be guilty of any form of misconduct,

to tackle early, or late, or dangerously, including the action known as 'a stiff arm tackle',
who is not running for the ball wilfully to charge or obstruct an opponent who has just kicked the ball,
to hold, push, charge, obstruct or grasp an opponent not holding the ball except in a scrummage, ruck or maul,

to commit any misconduct on the playing area which is prejudicial to the spirit of good sportsmanship.

MATCH CONTROL

REFEREE'S SIGNALS

Free kick

Try

Penalty

Throw-forward

Advantage

Scrummage

Knock-on

Match Control – Referee

Rugby is a physical game, full of movement, action and excitement. The game must be played to certain Laws, and it is necessary to have a neutral and unbiased person who has the authority to enforce those Laws – a referee.

Law 6 states 'There shall be a referee for every match ... the referee shall keep the time and the score and he must ... apply fairly the Laws of the Game'.

It is self-evident that the role of the referee in rugby is important. Without him there would be no game for the players. At the same time, a referee should remember that the game is for the players' benefit, and not for himself. A referee's approach, therefore, can influence a game, and how the players react. He must realise that his job is to control the *whole* match and not merely a series of individual incidents. To achieve this, the referee must set out to control matters from the first whistle, and he should let the players know exactly what he expects of them.

The correct approach should aim to achieve clarity, consistency and control.

CLARITY
Make clear to the players why the whistle has been blown. A clear signal and a brief explanation: 'Knock-on Reds, no advantage, scrummage here to Blues.'

CONSISTENCY
Maintain a uniform interpretation of the Laws for the duration of the game. Nothing is more irritating or upsetting to players than, for instance, being penalised for an offence and then a few minutes later seeing an opponent being allowed to get away unpenalised for the same offence. Both sides should be treated the same.

CONTROL
This is the referee's ability – through good management of players and by intelligent application of the Laws – to ensure that the game is played in a good spirit, without any misconduct, and within the Laws of the game. The referee must remember that he is there to apply the Laws fairly and to make decisions on Law in the game. The players must not make the decisions for him.

The Advantage Law (Law 8)

This is the shortest Law in the game, yet it is the most important, and probably the most difficult to interpret correctly. The referee is given a wide discretion as to what constitutes advantage immediately following an infringement; to the players the old statement 'keep playing until you hear the referee's whistle' is really the advantage law. A good referee, by wise and intelligent application of this Law, can attain continuity of play and ensure a flowing pattern to a game.

But when should the referee's whistle be blown following an infringement?

The timing and interpretation of the Advantage Law is left to the individual referee. Because of this very wide discretion it is important that the referee quickly achieves consistency in his own interpretation of the Advantage Law. In effect it is the one Law that can be played without blowing the whistle, and the better the application of this Law, the more enjoyable a game becomes.

It is a Law that a referee learns to interpret correctly with experience and by a good understanding of the game. However, during the learning process referees should never forget that they are the sole judges as to whether or not advantage has been gained.

REFEREE'S GUIDE

Every match produces a variety of situations and their resultant problems require instant and correct decisions. Only with a clear understanding of the game, and a good knowledge of the Laws, can a referee carry out his duties effectively.

In order to control the different situations which arise in a game, a referee should prepare himself with a logical sequence as to what he is looking for in each situation and how each individual problem can be solved. Referees should formulate *checklists* for every possible situation.

Here are a few examples of checklists.

Kit

1. Jerseys (3 colours)
2. Shorts
3. Socks
4. Boots
5. Laces
6. Hold-ups
7. Jock strap
8. Whistle (two at least)
9. Watch
10. Notebook
11. Pencils
12. Towel and soap
13. Safety pins
14. Liniment
15. Comb
16. First-aid kit

Pre-match

1. Kick-off time
2. Direction to ground and telephone number

3. Team colours
4. Competition rules
5. Changing room
6. Team room
7. Ground condition
8. Pitch markings and flags
9. Touch judges
10. Balls
11. Teams(?)
12. Toss
13. Captains
14. Stud inspection

Kick-off

1. Two touch judges
2. Two teams × 15
3. Who kicks off
4. Who selects ends
5. Ball
6. Are opponents ten metres away?
7. Are kicker's team behind ball?
8. Are opponent's team ready to receive?
9. Check watch
10. Blow whistle, kick-off
11. Be careful of switch kick – keep out of way

Tackle

1. Is it a tackle?
2. Is player carrying ball held by an opponent?
3. Is player carrying ball on the ground?
4. Has player carrying ball released the ball?
5. Is he attempting to roll clear of the ball or get on to his feet?
6. Is tackling player on ground?

7. Has tackling player released ball carrier?
8. Is tackling player rolling away?
9. Is tackling player back on his feet before playing ball?
10. Are other players attempting to play ball – not man?

Scrummage

1. Is correct place indicated?
2. Is correct team putting ball into scrummage?
3. Is scrum-half ready with ball in his hands?
4. Are both front rows individually bound?
5. Are lock-forwards bound?
6. Are the front rows square-on?
7. Are the opposing props bound correctly?
8. Are flankers bound properly?
9. Is scrum-half a metre from scrummage?
10. Was ball put into scrummage and hooked properly?
11. Is opposing scrum-half behind ball?
12. Are three-quarters on-side (swivel head)?
13. Is ball out of scrummage?

Line-out

1. Is ball in touch?
2. Was kick direct outside 22?
3. Is touch judge in correct place?

4. Has ball been touched by spectators, ball boys, etc?
5. Are there at least two players from both teams in line-out?
6. Are players between five and fifteen metre lines?
7. Are spaces between all players correct?
8. Are three-quarters on-side?
9. Is thrower-in behind touch-line?
10. Was ball 'straight' in line-out?
11. Were jumpers OK?
12. Has line-out ended?
13. Are three-quarters on-side?

Ruck

1. Is ball on ground?
2. Is there a player from both teams standing over ball?
3. Are players on feet in physical contact?
4. Are three-quarters on-side?
5. Is ball being played only with feet?
6. Are all players in ruck correctly bound?
7. Are players joining ruck from correct side, behind ball?
8. Is ball out of ruck?
9. Are three-quarters on-side?

Maul

1. Is ball held in player's hands?
2. Is there at least one player from both teams around ball carrier?

3. Are players joining maul from correct side, behind ball?
4. Are three-quarters on-side?
5. Are all players in maul in physical contact?
6. Are all players in maul standing on feet?
7. Is ball out of maul?
8. Are three-quarters on-side?

These checklists are not comprehensive. Referees should be encouraged to formulate their own checklists, and mentally refer to them during a match. They should be remembered as an aid to better refereeing. Referees should use checklists for other laws and situations, e.g. off-side/on-side, penalty kicks, free kicks, etc. A good checklist will help ensure good control.

Positioning

In order to apply the Laws of the game (via his checklists) a referee should be at all times in the best position to see everything taking place. This is an art which can only be acquired by observing other referees and by practice. The first aim of the referee must be to be up with play always, so that when a crucial decision needs to be taken he will be on the spot.

No two referees are built the same physically, and therefore there can be no 'right' position for all referees. Each referee must develop his own positioning skills, based on positions best suited to his ideas and physique. The following are pointers on positioning.

1. Keep moving, don't be left flat-footed at set-piece situations.
2. Try to keep in-field, but don't be

afraid to get touch-line side of ruck/maul.

3. Keep your checklists clearly in mind to be sure of the sequence of events to look for, especially at line-out, scrummage, ruck and maul.
4. Position yourself according to the checklist after locating the ball.
5. At line-out, scrummage, ruck and maul use the swivel head to check on players not involved in these situations.
6. Although immediate events are important, try to anticipate what is going to happen next, and position yourself accordingly.
7. Remember positioning is like watching TV: you take up the position which suits you best and which gives you the best view!

Decisions

Use your whistle, your signals and your word of mouth explanations so as to make your intentions and decisions clear and understandable to the players. The referee's decision is *final*.

PLAYER'S GUIDE

An understanding of the Laws, especially of those applicable to your playing position, will improve your play and add to your enjoyment of the game.

The Team

NO. 1	NO. 2	NO. 3
LOOSE-HEAD PROP	HOOKER	TIGHT-HEAD PROP
Laws 20, 21, 22, 23	Laws 20, 21, 22, 23	Laws 20, 21, 22, 23

NO. 4	NO. 5
LOCK-FORWARD	LOCK-FORWARD
Laws 20, 21, 22, 23	Laws 20, 21, 22, 23

NO. 6	NO. 8	NO. 7
FLANKER		FLANKER

Laws 18, 19, 20, 21, 22, 23, 24, 25

NO. 9
SCRUM-HALF
Laws 20, 23, 24, 25

NO. 10
OUTSIDE-HALF
Laws 24, 25

NO. 11	NO. 12	NO. 13	NO. 14
LEFT WING	LEFT CENTRE	RIGHT CENTRE	RIGHT WING

Laws 18, 24, 25

NO. 15
FULL-BACK
Laws 16, 18, 19, 24, 25

The Principles of Play

These four Principles of Play are basic to the game of rugby, and all players should be aware of their importance within the Laws of the game.

1. GO FORWARD – towards the opponents' goal-line.
2. SUPPORT – the player in your team who has the ball.
3. CONTINUITY – keep the ball 'alive'.
4. PRESSURE – on the opponents when they have the ball.

All the Laws are relevant to the players in a game of rugby, but players should know the fundamental Laws of off-side and on-side, Laws 24 and 25, remembering that in *open* play you cannot be off-side when an opponent has possession of the ball.

As well as a knowledge of the Laws, players should appreciate the essential techniques and skills required in certain situations – the *key factors* in getting it right.

Tackle – Law 18

KEY FACTORS – PLAY
1. Line up ball carrier.
2. Drive in your shoulders below opponent's waist.
3. Ensure your head is on opponent's buttocks.
4. Lock arms around opponent's legs.
5. Pull with your arms, push with your shoulder.
6. Bring opponent to ground, hold on tight.

KEY FACTORS – LAW
a. Only tackle ball carrier.
b. Once on ground tackled player must release ball and roll away.
c. Once on ground tackling player must release tackled player and roll away.
d. Players on ground after tackle cannot touch ball until back on their feet.

Ruck and Maul – Laws 21 and 22

KEY FACTORS – PLAY
1. Support the ball.
2. Body position: straight back, position shoulders above hips.
3. Drive forward, stay on feet.
4. Attitude and approach to win possession.

KEY FACTORS – LAW
a. Stay on feet, joining from your own side and behind the ball.
b. Physical contact required in maul, bind at least arm in ruck.
c. Players not in ruck/maul must stay behind off-side line – last foot.

Scrummage – Law 20

KEY FACTORS – PLAY
1. Foot position for correct support of scrummage and ball channel.
2. Body angle, straight back, position shoulders above hips.
3. Snap shove forward or lock out scrummage.
4. Drive forward.

KEY FACTORS – LAW
a. Stay on feet, play ball only with feet. Must be able to push forward.
b. All players must bind in scrummage, with at least one arm around body.
c. Scrum-half stands one metre from centre of scrum, puts ball in quickly without delay from between knee and ankle.
d. Outside players must stay behind off-side line – last foot.

Line-out – Law 23

KEY FACTORS – PLAY
1. Throw-in.
2. Catch/deflection, time of jump.
3. Support ball catcher.
4. Variation of line-out ploys.

KEY FACTORS – LAW
a. Correct space between all players in line-out. Line-out between five and fifteen metre lines.
b. Two players at least from each team.
c. Only jumpers to move before ball is touched.
d. Ball must be thrown five metres, alighting along line-of-touch.
e. Outside players must be ten metres away from line-of-touch.

The *key factors* of play are essential for effective performance in these areas, and the adherence of the *key factors* in Law are important for playing within the Laws.

Match Control

Law 6 provides the referee with wide powers to control a game. His decision, once made, cannot be altered, even if the referee realises that he has made a mistake. All players should respect the authority of the referee and accept his decisions.

Players should continue playing the game until they hear the referee's whistle to stop play. Players should be aware of the referee applying the Advantage Law (Law 8).

It must be remembered that rugby is a physical contact game, but that any action by a player which the referee deems dangerous, or foul play, will be severely punished and could result in the dismissal from the field of play of the offending player.

CLUB OFFICIALS' GUIDE

The officials of each club should understand their duties with regard to the game, and to the preservation of the good name of their club, and the game of rugby.

The club in turn is responsible for the conduct of all their players and officials. It is the duty of clubs and committees at all levels to refrain from selecting players who are continually guilty of foul play.

Duties

The home club is responsible for the welfare of the referee (and touch judges) before and after a match.

The club or Union in charge of the match arrangements is responsible for the following.
1. The correct marking of the playing area.
2. Providing the correct equipment, e.g. corner posts and flags, balls, etc.
3. Advising the referee of all details of the match including the location of the game, the time of kick-off, team colours and any other relevant information.
4. Providing suitable changing-room facilities for players and referee.
5. Preventing spectators from encroaching on to the playing area.
6. In any league or cup match, a club must have a copy of the relevant competition rules available for the referee, especially in the event of a drawn match.
7. Proper first-aid facilities, including a stretcher, should be available, and a medically trained person should be in attendance in case of injury.

All club officials, including the trainer and coach, should be instructed not to enter the field of play whilst a game is in progress, without the permission of the referee.

EXPERIMENTAL VARIATIONS TO THE LAWS OF THE GAME

In 1985 'Experimental Variations' to the Laws and Notes were introduced to be used by all Member Unions at all levels. The Laws thus affected are to be marked **E** in the margin of the Board's Handbook. We have also marked them in this way in Part II of this book. The Laws affected are 4, 6A, 18, 19, 20, 21, 22 and 26.

We reprint below the Board's explanation for the introduction of the Experimental Variations:

The 'Experimental Variations' are intended to minimise the possibility of accidental injury during the formation and setting of a scrummage and particularly to reduce the possibility of the front rows collapsing. A crouched position and a 'normal stance' are seen as important components of this intent and should be viewed as such. Although normal stance is not defined, it would involve a player facing his opponents squarely, being correctly bound, with shoulders not lower than hips, both feet on the ground and not crossed until the ball has been put in.

In considering this intention, the requirement of Law 14(b), that players in the front rows must not at any time during the scrummage wilfully adopt any position which is likely to cause the scrummage to collapse, should also be noted. With the Experimental Variations it is for the referee to decide, under the conditions applicable at the time, whether players may be 'likely to cause the scrummage to collapse' through the stance they adopt after the front rows have engaged.

PART II

Laws of the Game of RUGBY FOOTBALL

with **Instructions and Notes on the Laws**

As framed by the
International Rugby Football Board

FOREWORD

The Laws of the Game are complete and contain all that is necessary to enable the game to be played correctly and fairly. Nevertheless, in a complex game where so many diverse situations can arise, the Board finds it necessary to instruct all concerned as to the meaning and effect of some of the Laws, and to add emphasis to duties which the Laws place on the referee. This is all the more necessary because lack of uniformity in referees' decisions is bad for the game.

These Instructions and Notes are, therefore, issued by the International Rugby Football Board so that all concerned in every country may follow a consistent and uniform practice.

It is the duty of the referee (Law 6A(3)) to apply fairly the Laws of the Game without any variation or omission. Equally, the referee is obliged to follow the instructions and guide-lines herein laid down by the International Board.

OBJECT OF THE GAME

The Object of the Game is that two teams of fifteen players each, observing fair play according to the Laws and a sporting spirit, should by carrying, passing and kicking the ball score as many points as possible, the team scoring the greater number of points to be the winner of the match.

DECLARATION OF AMATEURISM

The Game is an amateur game. No-one is allowed to seek or to receive payment or other material reward for taking part in the Game.

DEFINITIONS

The following terms have the meaning assigned to them:

Beyond or **Behind** or **In front** of any position implies 'with both feet', except when unsuited to the context.

Dead means that the ball is for the time being out of play. This occurs when the referee blows his whistle to indicate a stoppage of play or when an attempt to convert a try is unsuccessful.

Defending Team means the team in whose half of the ground the stoppage of play occurs and the opponents of the defending team are referred to as '**the Attacking Team**'.

Kick. A kick is made by propelling the ball with any part of the leg or foot (except the heel), from knee to toe inclusive. If the player is holding the ball, he must propel it out of his hands or, if it is on the ground, he must propel it a visible distance.

Drop Kick. A drop kick is made by letting the ball fall from the hand (or hands) to the ground and kicking it at the first rebound as it rises.

Place Kick. A place kick is made by kicking the ball after it has been placed on the ground for that purpose.

Punt. A punt is made by letting the ball fall from the hand (or hands) and kicking it before it touches the ground.

Mark. The mark is the place at which a free kick or penalty kick is awarded.

Line Through the Mark (or Place). Except where specifically stated otherwise, the words 'a line through the mark' or 'a line through the place' always means a line parallel to the touch line.

Union means the controlling body under whose jurisdiction the match is played and in the case of an International Match it means the International Rugby Football Board or a Committee thereof.

Other definitions are included in and have effect as part of the Laws.

THE LAWS

LAW 1 Ground

The field-of-play is the area as shown on the plan, bounded by, but not including, the goal lines and touch lines.

The **playing area** *is the field-of-play and In-goal.*

The **playing enclosure** *is the playing area and a reasonable area surrounding it.*

The **Plan,** including all words and figures thereon, is to take effect as part of these Laws.

The **Terms** appearing on the Plan are to bear their apparent meaning and to be deemed part of the definitions as if separately included.

(1) All lines shown on the plan must be suitably marked out. The touch lines are in touch. The goal lines are in In-goal. The dead-ball line is **not** in In-goal. The touch-in-goal lines and corner posts are in touch-in-goal. The goal posts are to be erected in the goal lines.

(2) The game must be played on a ground of the area (maximum) shown on the plan and marked in accordance with the plan. The surface must be grass-covered or, where this is not available, clay or sand provided the surface is not of dangerous hardness.

Note: (1) Advertising painted on the surface of the playing area is not permitted.

NOTES

⌐ *Indicates post with flag.*

Length and breadth of field to be as near to dimensions indicated as possible. All areas to be rectangular.

— — — — — These broken lines indicate 10 metres distance from the half-way line and 5 metres distance from the touch lines.

———————— These lines at the goal lines and intersecting the 22 metres and 10 metres lines and the half-way line are 15 metres from the touch lines. The lines at the goal lines extend 5 metres into the field-of-play.

Goal dimensions: 3.00 metres is taken from the ground to the top edge of the crossbar and 5.60 metres from inside to inside of the goal posts.

A minimum height of 1.20 metres above the ground is desirable for corner posts.

(3) Any objection by the visiting team about the ground or the way in which it is marked out must be made to the referee before the first kick-off.

THE PLAN

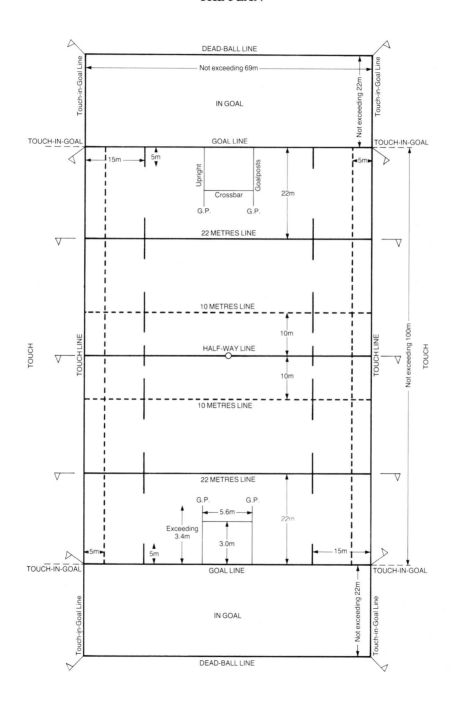

LAW 2 Ball

(1) The ball when new shall be oval in shape, of four panels and of the following dimensions:

Length in line 280 to 300 mm
Circumference (end on) 760 to 790 mm
Circumference (in width) 580 to 620 mm
Weight 400 to 440 gms

Note: (1) The ball, at commencement of play, should have a pressure equivalent to $9\frac{1}{2}$–10 lb. per square inch (0.6697–0.7031 kilograms per square centimetre) at sea level.

(2) The dimensions of the ball may be reduced only for younger schoolboys.

(3) Balls may be specially treated to make them resistant to mud and easier to grip. The casings need not be of leather.

Note: (2) It is permissible to have spare balls available during a match, but a team may not gain or attempt to gain an unfair advantage through their use or by changing them.

LAW 3 Number of Players

(1) A match shall be played by not more than fifteen players in each team.

(2) Replacement of players shall be allowed in recognized trial matches as determined by the Union having jurisdiction over the match.

(3) In all other matches, a player may be replaced only on account of injury and subject to the following conditions:

(a) Not more than two players in each team may be replaced.

Exception: In matches between teams of schoolboys or teams where all players are under the age of 19, up to six players may be replaced.

(b) A player who has been replaced must NOT resume playing in the match.

(4) (a) In matches in which a national representative team is playing, a player may be replaced ONLY when, in the opinion of a medical practitioner, the player is so injured that he should not continue playing in the match.

(b) For such competition and other domestic matches as a Union gives express permission, an injured player may be replaced—
● on the advice of a medically trained person, or
● if a medically trained person is not present, with the approval of the referee.

(5) If the referee is advised by a doctor or other medically trained person or for any other reason considers that a player is so injured that it would be harmful for him to continue playing, the referee shall require the player to leave the playing area.

(6) Any objection by either team as regards the number of players in a team may be made to the referee at any time but objections shall not affect any score previously obtained.

Note: (1) As soon as a referee becomes aware that a team has more than the correct number of players on the field, he must require the captain of that team to reduce the number of players appropriately.

Attention is drawn to the Resolution adopted by the Board which states that 'A player who has suffered definite concussion should not participate in any match or training session for a period of at least three weeks from the time of injury, and then only subject to being cleared by a proper neurological examination'.

LAW 4 Players' Dress

(1) A player must not wear dangerous projections such as buckles or rings.
(2) Shoulder pads of the 'harness' type must not be worn. If the referee is satisfied that a player requires protection following an injury to a shoulder, the wearing of a pad of cottonwool, sponge rubber or similar soft material may be permitted provided the pad is attached to the body or sewn on to the jersey.
(3) Studs of a player's boots must conform to the British Standard BS 6366: 1983. They must be circular, securely fastened to the boots and of the following dimensions:

Maximum length (measured from sole)	18 mm
Minimum diameter at base	13 mm
Minimum diameter at top	10 mm
Minimum diameter of washer (if separate from stud)	20 mm

The wearing of a single stud at the toe of the boot is prohibited.
(4) The referee has power to decide before or during the match that any part of a player's dress is dangerous. He must then order the player to remove the dangerous part and permit him to resume playing in the match only after it has been removed.

LAW 5 Toss, Time

No-side is the end of a match.
(1) Before a match begins the captains shall toss for the right to kick-off or the choice of ends.
(2) The duration of play in a match shall be such time not exceeding eighty minutes as shall be directed by the Union or, in the absence of such direction, as agreed upon by the teams or, if not agreed, as fixed by the referee. In International matches two periods of forty minutes each shall be played.

Note: (1) The term 'not exceeding eighty minutes' excludes any extra time which the Union may direct or authorise to be played in the case of a drawn match in a knock-out competition.

(3) Play shall be divided into two halves. At half-time the teams shall change ends and there shall be an interval of not more than five minutes.

(4) A period not exceeding one minute shall be allowed for treatment of an injury to a player or for any other permitted delay. A longer period may be allowed only if the additional time is required for the removal of an injured player from the playing area.

Playing time lost as a result of any such permitted delay or of delay in taking a kick at goal shall be made up in that half of the match in which the delay occurred, subject to the power vested in the referee to declare no-side before time has expired.

Note: (2) The referee must make up time lost through any delay in taking a kick at goal. This applies whether or not the referee considers the delay to be 'undue delay' on the part of the kicker. Playing time lost should begin from 40 seconds after the player has indicated his intention to kick at goal.

LAW 6 Referee and Touch Judges

A. Referee

(1) There shall be a referee for every match. He shall be appointed by or under the authority of the Union or, in case no such authorised referee has been appointed, a referee may be mutually agreed upon between the teams or, failing such agreement, he shall be appointed by the home team.

(2) If the referee is unable to officiate for the whole period of a match a replacement shall be appointed either in such manner as may be directed by the Union or, in the absence of such direction, by the referee or, if he is unable to do so, by the home team.

(3) The referee shall keep the time and the score, and he must in every match apply fairly the Laws of the Game without any variation or omission, except only when the Union has authorised the application of an experimental law approved by the International Board.

Notes: (1) If the referee is in doubt as to the correct time he should consult either or both of the touch judges. Only if the information given by them is insufficient may he consult another person.

(2) Where the referee allows time for delays the time must be made up in the half of the match in which the delay occurs.

(3) The referee has power to declare no-side before time has expired if, in his opinion, the full time cannot for any reason be played or continuance of play would be dangerous.

(4) Where a player is injured, the referee should not allow more than one minute delay unless a longer period is necessary to remove the player, or to give essential treatment on the playing area.

(5) The referee should not allow time for injury if he has reason to believe that a player is feigning injury. In such circumstances he should order the player to be removed immediately from the playing area and then order play to be resumed forthwith.

(6) The referee should, when the ball is dead, allow time for a player to replace or repair a badly torn jersey or shorts. He must not allow time for a player to re-tie or repair a bootlace.

(4) He must not give any instruction or advice to either team prior to the match. During the match he must not consult with anyone except only

(a) either or both touch judges on a point of fact relevant to their functions, or on matters relating to Law 26(3), or

(b) in regard to time.

(5) The referee is the sole judge of fact and of law. All his decisions are binding on the players. He cannot alter a decision except when given before he observes that a touch judge's flag is raised or before he has received a report related to Law 26(3) from a touch judge.

(6) The referee must carry a whistle and must blow it

(a) to indicate the beginning of the match, half-time, resumption of play after half-time, no-side, a score or a touch-down, and

(b) to stop play because of infringement or otherwise as required by the Laws.

Notes: (7) The referee has power to stop the match at any time by blowing his whistle but he must not do so except on the occasions indicated in Law 6A(6) which include the following:

(a) when he orders a scrummage;

(b) when the ball has gone into touch or touch-in-goal, or touched or crossed the dead-ball lines;

(c) when the ball has been grounded in In-goal;

(d) when the ball is unplayable;

(e) when he stops play for an offence under Law 26(3) prior to ordering off or cautioning the offender; and in such a case he must whistle a second time when he awards the penalty try or kick;

(f) when he awards a penalty kick or free kick;

(g) when he allows a fair-catch;

(h) when the ball or a player carrying it has touched him and one team has therefrom gained an advantage;

(i) when a player is injured but only when the ball next becomes dead unless (j) below applies;

(j) when continuance of play would be dangerous, including the collapse of a scrummage.

(8) The referee should whistle for half-time or no-side as soon as time has expired if the ball be dead or if the ball be in play when the time has expired, as soon as the ball next becomes dead.

If the ball becomes dead after time has expired

(a) as the result of a try the referee shall allow the kick to be taken and then whistle for half-time or no-side, or if it be

(b) as the result of a fair-catch, free kick or penalty kick the referee shall allow play to proceed until the ball next becomes dead.

If time expires before the ball is put into a scrummage or is thrown in from touch, the referee **must** whistle for half-time or no-side.

(7) During a match no person other than the players, the referee and the touch judges may be within the playing enclosure or the playing area unless with the permission of the referee which shall be given only for a special and temporary purpose.

Note: (9) The referee should, when necessary, but not before he indicates his permission, allow baggage attendants and doctors or first aid personnel to enter the playing enclosure and playing area. He should be strict in refusing permission to persons intending to give advice or instructions to a team, and players should not be allowed to leave the playing area to get advice or instructions. Latitude should, however, be allowed in recognised trial matches.

(8) (a) All players must respect the authority of the referee and they must not dispute his decisions. They must (except in the case of a kick-off) stop playing at once when the referee has blown his whistle.

(b) A player must when so requested, whether before or during the match, allow the referee to inspect his dress.

(c) A player must not leave the playing enclosure without the referee's permission. If player retires during a match because of injury or otherwise, he must not resume playing in that match until the referee has given him permission.

Notes: (10) Apart from injury the referee should not allow a player to leave the playing enclosure except in special circumstances.

The referee should not permit a player to resume until the ball is dead.

(11) The referee must not permit a team or individual players to leave the playing area in order to change jerseys.

(12) If a player who has retired on account of injury or other reason resumes playing without the permission of the referee, the referee should impose penalties for misconduct if he considers that the offence was wilful for the purpose of assisting his team or obstructing the opponents. If the offence was not wilful interference and if the offending team gains an advantage the referee should order a scrummage at the place where the player resumed playing without permission, and the opposing team shall put in the ball.

Penalty: Infringement by a player is subject to penalty as misconduct.

B. Touch Judges

(1) There shall be two touch judges for every match. Unless touch judges have been appointed by or under the authority of the Union, it shall be the responsibility of each team to provide a touch judge.

(2) A touch judge is under the control of the referee who may instruct him as to his duties and may over-rule any of his decisions. The referee may request that an unsatisfactory touch judge be replaced and he has power to order off and report to the Union a touch judge who in his opinion is guilty of misconduct.

(3) Each touch judge shall carry a flag (or other suitable object) to signal his decisions. There shall be one touch judge on each side of the ground and he shall remain in touch except when judging a kick at goal.

(4) He must hold up his flag when the ball or a player carrying it has gone into touch and must indicate the place of throw-in and which team is entitled to do so. He must also signal to the referee when the ball or a player carrying it has gone into touch-in-goal.

(5) The touch judge shall lower his flag when the ball has been thrown in except on the following occasions when he must keep it raised:
  (a) when the player throwing in the ball puts any part of either foot in the field-of-play,
  (b) when the ball has not been thrown in by the team entitled to do so,
  (c) when, at a quick throw-in, the ball that went into touch is replaced by another or is handled by anyone other than the players.

It is for the referee to decide whether or not the ball has been thrown in from the correct place.

(6) In matches in which a national representative team is playing and in such domestic matches for which a Union gives express permission, and where referees recognised by the Union are appointed as touch judges, the touch judges may report incidents of foul play and misconduct under Law 26(3) to the referee for the match.

A touch judge may signal such an incident to the referee by raising his flag to a horizontal position pointing in the direction of the goal-line of the offending team. The touch judge must remain in touch and continue to carry out his other functions until the next stoppage in play when the referee shall consult him regarding the incident. The referee may then take whatever action he deems appropriate and any consequent penalties shall be in accordance with Law 26 (3).

(7) When a kick at goal from a try or penalty kick is being taken both touch judges must assist the referee by signalling the result of the kick. One touch judge shall stand at or behind each of the goal posts and shall raise his flag if the ball goes over the cross-bar.

LAW 7 Mode of Play

A match is started by a kick-off, after which any player who is on-side may at any time

- catch or pick up the ball and run with it,
- pass, throw or knock the ball to another player,
- kick or otherwise propel the ball,

- tackle, push or shoulder an opponent holding the ball,
- fall on the ball,
- take part in scrummage, ruck, maul or line-out

provided he does so in accordance with these Laws.

Note: (1) If a player hands the ball to another player of his team without any propulsion or throwing of the ball, this does constitute a pass.

LAW 8 Advantage

The referee shall not whistle for an infringement during play which is followed by an advantage gained by the non-offending team. An advantage must be either territorial or such possession of the ball as constitutes an obvious tactical advantage. A mere opportunity to gain advantage is not sufficient.

Notes: (1) The referee is given a wide discretion as to what constitutes an advantage and is not limited to a territorial advantage. The referee is the sole judge of whether an advantage has been gained.

(2) The **only** occasions when advantage does not apply are:
(a) when the ball or a player carrying it touches the referee (Law 9(1));
(b) when the ball emerges from either end of the tunnel at a scrummage not having been played (Law 20, note (10));

(c) when a player is 'accidentally off-side' (Exception (i), Law 24(A) (2) (b)).

(3) When any irregularity of play not provided for in the Laws occurs, a scrummage shall be formed where the irregularity occurred. In deciding which team should put in the ball, the referee should apply Law 20(7).

LAW 9 Ball or Player Touching Referee

(1) If the ball or a player carrying it touches the referee in the field-of-play, play shall continue unless the referee considers either team has gained an advantage in which case he shall order a scrummage. The team which last played the ball shall put it in.

(2) (a) If the ball in a player's possession or a player carrying it touches the referee in that player's In-goal, a touch-down shall be awarded.

(b) If a player carrying the ball in his opponents' In-goal touches the referee before grounding the ball, a try shall be awarded at that place.

Notes: (1) If the ball, while in play in In-goal at either end but not held by a player, touches the referee, a touch judge, or a spectator, a touch-down shall be awarded provided that a touch-down would otherwise have been obtained or the ball would have gone into touch-in-goal or on or over the dead-ball line.

(2) If the ball while in play in In-goal at either end, but not held by a player, touches the referee, a touch judge, or a spectator, a try shall be awarded at that place provided an attacking player would otherwise have scored it.

(3) When the ball touches a spectator in either of the above cases, if the referee is in doubt, the award shall be made to the visiting team if that team is the defending team under (1) or the attacking team under (2).

LAW 10 Kick-off

Kick-off is (a) a place kick taken from the centre of the half-way line by the team which has the right to start the match or by the opposing team on the resumption of play after the half-time interval or by the defending team after a goal has been scored, or (b) a drop-kick taken at or from behind the centre of the half-way line by the defending team after an unconverted try.

(1) The ball must be kicked from the correct place and by the correct form of kick; otherwise it shall be kicked off again.

(2) The ball must reach the opponents' ten metres line, unless first played by an opponent; otherwise it shall be kicked off again, or a scrummage formed at the centre, at the opponents' option. If it reaches the ten metres line and is then blown back, play shall continue.

(3) If the ball pitches directly into touch, touch-in goal or over or on the dead-ball line, the opposing team may accept the kick, have the ball kicked off again, or have a scrummage formed at the centre.

(4) The **kicker's team** must be behind the ball when kicked; otherwise a scrummage shall be formed at the centre.

(5) The **opposing team** must stand on or behind the ten metres line. If they are in front of that line or if they charge before the ball has been kicked, it shall be kicked off again.

LAW 11 Method of Scoring

Try. A try is scored by first grounding the ball in the opponents' In-goal.

A try shall be awarded if one would probably have been scored but for foul play by the opposing team.

Goal. A goal is scored by kicking the ball over the opponents' crossbar and between the goal posts from the field-of-play by any place kick or drop kick, except a kick-off, drop-out or free kick, without touching the ground or any player of the kicker's team.

A goal is scored if the ball has crossed the bar, even though it may have been blown backwards afterwards, and whether it has touched the crossbar or either goal post or not.

A goal is scored if the ball has crossed the bar notwithstanding a prior offence of the opposing team.

A goal may be awarded if the ball is illegally touched by any player of the opposing team and if the referee considers that a goal would otherwise probably have been scored.

The scoring values are as follows:

A try	4 points
A goal scored after a try	2 points
A goal from a penalty kick	3 points
A dropped goal otherwise obtained	3 points

LAW 12 Try and Touch-down

Grounding the ball is the act of a player who
(a) *while holding the ball in his hand (or hands) or arm (or arms) brings the ball in contact with the ground, or*
(b) *while the ball is on the ground either*
 ● *places his hand (or hands) or arm (or arms) on it with downward pressure, or*
 ● *falls upon it and the ball is anywhere under the front of his body from waist to neck inclusive.*
Picking up the ball from the ground is not grounding it.

A. Try

(1) A player who is on-side scores a try when
- he carries the ball into his opponents' In-goal, or
- the ball is in his opponents' In-goal, and he first grounds it there.

(2) The scoring of a try includes the following cases:
  (a) if a player carries, passes, knocks or kicks the ball into his In-goal and an opponent first grounds it,
  (b) if, at a scrummage or ruck, a team is pushed over its goal line and before the ball has emerged it is first grounded in In-goal by an attacking player,
  (c) if the momentum of a player, when tackled, carries him into his opponents' In-goal and he first there grounds the ball,
  (d) if a player first grounds the ball on his opponents' goal line or if the ball is in contact with the ground and a goal post.

(3) If a player grounds the ball in his opponents' In-goal and picks it up again, a try is scored where it was first grounded.

(4) A try may be scored by a player who is in touch or in touch-in-goal provided he is not carrying the ball.

B. Penalty Try

A penalty try shall be awarded between the posts if but for foul play by the defending team
- a try would probably have been scored, or
- it would probably have been scored in a more favourable position than that where the ball was grounded.

C. Touch-Down

(1) A touch-down occurs when a player first grounds the ball in his In-goal.

(2) After a touch-down, play shall be re-started either by a drop-out or a scrummage, as provided in Law 14.

D. Scrummage after Grounding in Case of Doubt

Where there is doubt as to which team first grounded the ball in In-goal, a scrummage shall be formed five metres from the goal line opposite the place where the ball was grounded. The attacking team shall put in the ball.

LAW 13 Kick at Goal after a Try

(1) After a try has been scored, the scoring team has the right to take a place kick or drop kick at goal, on a line through the place where the try was scored.
   If the scoring team does not take the kick, play shall be re-started by a drop kick from the centre, unless time has expired.

(2) If a kick is taken:
  (a) it must be taken without undue delay;
  (b) any player including the kicker may place the ball;
  (c) the **kicker's team,** except a placer, must be behind the ball when kicked;
  (d) if the kicker kicks the ball from a placer's hands without the ball being on the ground, the kick is void;
  (e) the **opposing team** must be behind the goal line until the kicker

begins his run or offers to kick when they may charge or jump with a view to preventing a goal.

(3) Neither the kicker nor a placer shall wilfully do anything which may lead the opposing team to charge prematurely. If either does so, the charge shall not be disallowed.

Penalty: ● **For an infringement by the *kicker's team* - the kick shall be disallowed.**

● **For an infringement by the *opposing team* - the charge shall be disallowed. If, however, the kick has been taken successfully, the goal shall stand. If it was unsuccessful, the kicker may take another kick under the original conditions without the charge and may change the type of kick.**

Notes: (1) In addition to the general provision regarding waste of time, the kicker is bound to kick without delay, under penalty.

A player should not be permitted to be unreasonably slow in taking any kick at goal. A period of one minute between the indication of intention to kick at goal and the actual kick is well inside the zone of 'undue delay'. A player who is unreasonably slow should be warned that if he persists in delay, penalties will be applied.

Even without a caution, if the delay is clearly a breach of law, the kick should be disallowed and a kick-off ordered.

(2) The referee must always make up time lost by any delay in taking the kick, as is provided for in note (2) under Law 5.

(3) The referee should see that the opposing players do not gradually creep up and that they have both feet behind the goal line, otherwise he should disallow the charge.

(4) Shouting by the defending team during a kick at goal should be treated as misconduct and, if no goal is scored, another kick should be allowed without the charge.

(5) When another kick is allowed for any reason, all the original preliminaries may be retaken.

(6) If the ball rolls over and away from the line through the place where the try was scored and the ball is kicked over the crossbar, a goal should be awarded.

(7) If, after the kicker has commenced his run, the ball rolls over into touch, another kick under the original conditions should **not** be allowed.

(8) The kick must be taken with the ball which was in play unless the referee decides that the ball is defective.

(9) The law does not allow the use of sand or sawdust for placing the ball on hard playing fields when taking a place kick at goal, but in exceptional local conditions, such a varia-

tion from normal practice might be permitted.

LAW 14 In-Goal

In-goal is the area bounded by a goal line, touch-in-goal lines and dead-ball line. It includes the goal line and goal posts but excludes touch-in-goal lines and dead-ball line.

Touch-in-goal occurs when the ball or a player carrying it touches a corner post or a touch-in-goal line or the ground or a person or object on or beyond it. The flag is not part of the corner post.

FIVE METRES SCRUMMAGE

(1) If a player carrying the ball in In-goal is so held that he cannot ground the ball, a scrummage shall be formed five metres from the goal line opposite the place where he was held.
The attacking team shall put in the ball.

(2) (a) If a defending player heels, kicks, carries, passes or knocks the ball over his goal line and it there becomes dead except where
  ● a try is scored, or
  ● he wilfully knocks or throws the ball from the field-of-play into touch-in-goal or over his dead-ball line, or
(b) if a defending player in In-goal has his kick charged down by an attacking player after
  ● he carried the ball back from the field-of-play, or
  ● a defending player put it into In-goal and the ball is then touched down or goes into touch-in-goal or over the dead-ball line, or

(c) if a defending player carrying the ball in the field-of-play is forced into his In-goal and he then touches down, or
(d) if, at a scrummage or ruck, a defending team with the ball in its possession is pushed over its goal line and before the ball has emerged first grounds it in In-goal,

a scrummage shall be formed five metres from the goal line opposite the place where the ball or a player carrying it crossed the goal line.
The attacking team shall put in the ball.

Notes: (1) If a defending player wilfully puts the ball back into his own In-goal, he accepts **all** the consequences of taking that action. Many things may happen in In-goal after the ball has been carried, passed, knocked, heeled or kicked back by a defending player and it may be quite an appreciable time before the ball becomes dead and Law 14 applies.

(2) Paragraph 2 (b) of Law 14 applies whether the attacking player charges down the kick in the field-of-play or in In-goal.

(3) If play similar to a maul takes place in In-goal, Law 14(1) applies.

DROP-OUT

(3) Except where the ball is knocked-on or thrown-forward or a try or goal is scored, if an attacking player kicks,

carries or passes the ball and it travels into his opponents' In-goal either directly or after having touched a defender who does not wilfully attempt to stop, catch or kick it, and it is there
● grounded by a player of **either** team, or
● goes into touch-in-goal or over the dead-ball line
a drop-out shall be awarded.

Penalties: (a) **A penalty try shall be awarded when by foul play in In-goal the defending team has prevented a try which otherwise would *probably* have been scored.**

(b) **A try shall be disallowed and a drop-out awarded, if a try would *probably not* have been gained but for foul play by the attacking team.**

(c) **For foul play in In-goal while the ball is out of play the penalty kick shall be awarded at the place where play would otherwise have re-started and, in addition, the player shall either be ordered off or cautioned that he will be sent off if he repeats the offence.**

(d) **For wilfully charging or obstructing in In-goal a player who has just kicked the ball the penalty shall be**

● **a drop-out, or, at the option of the non-offending team,**
● **a penalty kick where the ball alights as provided for an infringement of Law 26 (3) (d).**

(e) **For other infringements in In-goal, the penalty shall be:**
● **for an offence by the *attacking team* – a drop-out,**
● **for an offence by the *defending team* – a scrummage five metres from the goal line opposite the place of infringement.**

Notes: (4) The decisions open to the referee for infringements in In-goal are:

(a) For an offence by the attacking team:
   (i) a drop-out, or
   (ii) warning and/or sending off the player for foul play, or
   (iii) a penalty kick for foul play in In-goal while the ball is out of play.

(b) For an offence by the defending team:
   (i) a five metres scrummage, or
   (ii) a penalty try, or
   (iii) warning and/or sending off the player for foul play, or
   (iv) a penalty kick for foul

play in In-goal while the ball is out of play.

(5) A penalty kick must **not** be awarded for an offence in In-goal except **only** when either Law 14 Penalty (d) or Law 26 (3) (h) applies. In the latter case the penalty kick is to be taken either at the twenty-two metres line (at any point the non-offending team may select) or at the centre of the half-way line, whichever is the place where play would restart.

(6) If from a free kick or a penalty kick taken in In-goal the ball is made dead by the defending team before it has crossed the goal line, a scrummage shall be awarded to the attacking team five metres from the goal line opposite to where it was made dead.

LAW 15 Drop-out

A drop-out is a drop kick awarded to the defending team.

(1) The drop kick must be taken from anywhere on or behind the twenty-two metres line; otherwise the ball shall be dropped out again.

(2) The ball must reach the twenty-two metres line; otherwise the opposing team may have it dropped out again, or have a scrummage formed at the centre of the twenty-two metres line. If it reaches the twenty-two metres line and is then blown back, play shall continue.

Note: (1) If the ball does not reach the twenty-two metres line and an opponent picks up the ball and grounds it over the kicker's goal line, a try should be awarded.

(3) If the ball pitches directly into touch, the opposing team may accept the kick, have the ball dropped out again, or have a scrummage formed at the centre of the twenty-two metres line.

(4) The **kicker's team** must be behind the ball when kicked; otherwise a scrummage shall be formed at the centre of the twenty-two metres line.

(5) The **opposing team** must not charge over the twenty-two metres line; otherwise the ball shall be dropped out again.

Notes: (2) If a player of the opposing team remains beyond or crosses the twenty-two metres line for the purpose of delaying or interfering with the player who is about to drop-out, a penalty under Law 26 (3)(h) should be awarded.

(3) The advantage law applies where the drop kick does not reach the twenty-two metres line and goes into touch.

LAW 16 Fair-catch (Mark)

(a) *A player makes a fair-catch when being stationary with both feet on the ground on his side of his twenty-two metres line he cleanly catches the ball direct from a kick, knock-on or throw-forward by one of his opponents and, at the same time, he exclaims 'Mark!'*

A fair-catch may be obtained even though the ball on its way touches a goal post or crossbar and can be made in In-goal.

(b) *A free kick is awarded for a fair-catch.*

(1) The kick must be taken by the player making the fair-catch, unless he is injured in so doing. If he is unable to take the kick within one minute a scrummage shall be formed at the mark. His team shall put in the ball.

(2) If the mark is in In-goal, any resultant scrummage shall be five metres from the goal line on a line through the mark.

Notes: (1) 'His side of his twenty-two metres line' means that no part of either foot is on or beyond his twenty-two metres line.

(2) If an opponent unfairly charges the catcher in the field-of-play after the referee has blown his whistle for a fair-catch, a penalty kick shall be awarded. If the charge occurs in In-goal, a drop-out shall be awarded.

LAW 17 Knock-on or Throw-forward

A knock-on occurs when the ball travels forward towards the direction of the opponents' dead-ball line after:

● *a player loses possession of it, or*
● *a player propels or strikes it with his hand or arm, or*

● *it strikes a player's hand or arm.*

A throw-forward occurs when a player carrying the ball throws or passes it in the direction of his opponents' dead-ball line. A throw-in from touch is not a throw-forward. If the ball is not thrown or passed forward but it bounces forward after hitting a player or the ground, it is not a throw-forward.

Notes: (1) A pass, throw or knock-on should not be adjudged an infringement unless it is clearly so under the Law. If there is any doubt, play should be allowed to proceed.

(2) A fair-catch can be made from a knock-on.

(1) The knock-on or throw-forward must not be **intentional.**

Penalty: Penalty kick at the place of infringement.

(2) If the knock-on or throw-forward is **unintentional,** a scrummage shall be formed either at the place of infringement or, if it occurs at a line-out, fifteen metres from the touch line along the line-of-touch unless:

● a fair catch has been allowed, or
● the ball is knocked on by a player who is in the act of charging down the kick of an opponent but is not attempting to catch the ball, or
● the ball is knocked on one or more times by a player who is in the act of catching or picking it up or losing possession of it is recovered by that player before it has touched the ground or another player.

Note: (3) If an attacking player knocks-on or throws-forward in the field-of-play and the ball travels into In-goal, either directly or after having touched a defender who does not wilfully attempt to stop, catch or kick it, and it is there

(a) grounded by a player of either team,

or

(b) goes into touch-in-goal or over the dead-ball line,

a scrummage should be awarded at the place of the knock-on or throw-forward.

LAW 18 Tackle

A tackle occurs when a player carrying the ball in the field-of-play is held by one or more opponents so that while he is so held he is brought to the ground or the ball comes into contact with the ground. If the ball carrier is on one knee, or both knees, or is sitting on the ground, or is on top of another player who is on the ground, the ball carrier is deemed to have been brought to the ground.

(1) A tackled player must play the ball immediately or, if unable to play it, must release it immediately and get up or move away from it. He must not play the ball again or interfere with it in any way until he is on his feet. Any other player must:

- be on his feet before he can play the ball,
- not fall on or over a player lying on the ground with the ball in his possession,
- not fall on or over players lying on the ground with the ball between them or in close proximity.

Notes: (1) The requirement to play or release the ball immediately allows a player to put the ball on the ground in any direction, or to his side, provided he does so as soon as the tackle occurs. A tackled player is permitted to pass or throw the ball or push it along the ground provided he does so immediately and it is not in a forward direction.

(2) It is not a tackle if the ball carrier is lifted by an opponent so that both his feet are off the ground.

(3) If a tackled player does not play or release the ball immediately and the referee is in doubt as to responsibility for failure to play or release it, he should **at once** order a scrummage.

(2) It is illegal for any player:

- to prevent a tackled player from playing or releasing the ball, or getting up after he has played or released it, or
- to pull the ball from a tackled player's possession or attempt to pick up the ball before the tackled player has released it, or
- while lying on the ground after a tackle to play or interfere with the

77

ball in any way or to tackle or attempt to tackle an opponent carrying the ball.

Penalty: Penalty kick at the place of infringement.

(3) If a player carrying the ball is thrown or knocked over but not tackled, he may pass the ball or get up and continue his run even though the ball has touched the ground.

(4) A try may be scored if the momentum of a player carries him into his opponents' In-goal even though he is tackled.

Notes: (4) A ruck has been formed if players of both teams are in physical contact in close proximity around the ball on the ground after a tackle. If the ball is played with the hands or picked up before it emerges from the ruck, a penalty kick should be awarded.

(5) Danger may arise if a tackled player fails to play or release or roll away from the ball **at once** or is prevented from doing so. **In such cases the referee should not delay in awarding a penalty kick.**

(6) A player on one knee or both knees or sitting on the ground is deemed to be lying on the ground.

❸

LAW 19 Lying With, On or Near the Ball

(1) A player who has not been tackled but who is lying on the ground and hold-

ing the ball must **immediately** pass or release the ball or roll away from it or get up on his feet.

(2) A player or players lying on the ground in close proximity to the ball must not prevent an opponent gaining possession of it.

(3) A player or players from either team must not *wilfully* fall on or over a player who is lying on the ground with the ball in his possession or in close proximity, or on players lying on the ground with the ball between them.

❸

(4) A player must not fall on or over the ball emerging from a scrummage or ruck.

Penalty: Penalty kick at the place of infringement.

Notes: (1) A player on one knee or both knees or sitting on the ground is deemed to be lying on the ground.

(2) Advantage shall be played only if it occurs immediately.

❸

LAW 20 Scrummage

A scrummage, which can take place only in the field-of-play, is formed by players from each team closing up in readiness to allow the ball to be put on the ground between them but is not to be formed within five metres of the touch-line.

The middle player in each front row is the hooker, and the players on either side of him are the props.

The middle line means an imaginary line on the ground directly beneath the line formed by the junction of the shoulders of the two front rows.

Note: If the ball in a scrummage is on or over the goal line the scrummage is ended.

FORMING A SCRUMMAGE

(1) A team must not wilfully delay the forming of a scrummage.

(2) Every scrummage shall be formed at the place of infringement or as near thereto as is practicable within the field-of-play. It must be stationary with the middle line parallel to the goal lines until the ball has been put in.

E Before commencing engagement each front row must be in a crouched position with their heads and shoulders no lower than their hips and so that they are no more than one arm's length from their opponents' shoulders.

Notes: (1) To the extent that is necessary, the scrummage is to be moved from the place of infringement so that when it is near a goal line, the line of the front row of the defending team is in the field-of-play before the ball is put in. The scrummage is ended if the ball in the scrummage touches or crosses a goal line.

(2) When the place of infringement is within five metres of a touch-line the scrummage is to be formed five metres from that touch-line.

(3) It is dangerous play for a front row to form down some distance from its opponents and rush against them.

(4) A minimum of five players from each team shall be required to form a scrummage. Each front row of a scrummage shall have three players in it **at all times**. The head of a player in a front row shall not be next to the head of a player of the same team.

E While a scrummage is forming and is taking place, the shoulders of each player in the front row must not be lower than his hips. All players in each front row must adopt a normal stance. Both feet must be on the ground and, until the ball has been correctly put in, must not be crossed. A hooker's foot must not be in front of the forward feet of his props.

Notes: (3) The referee should not permit the front rows to close up until the ball is in the hands of the player putting in the ball and is available to be put in immediately.

E A crouched position is the extension of the normal stance by bending the knees sufficiently to step into the engagement without a charge.

(4) The restriction on the crossing of the feet of the players in the front rows refers only to the feet of individual players; but the feet of **all** players in the front rows 'must be in the position for an effective forward shove'.

(5) A flank forward in the second or third row of a scrummage may pack at an angle provided

79

he is properly bound. If the ball is emerging from the back of the scrummage and he moves outwards, thereby preventing an opponent from advancing around the scrummage, a penalty kick should be awarded.

In the event of a scrummage collapsing the referee should whistle immediately so that players do not continue to push.

E

BINDING OF PLAYERS

(6) (a) The players of each front row shall bind firmly and continuously while the scrummage is forming, while the ball is being put in and while it is in the scrummage.

E

(b) The hooker may bind either over or under the arms of his props but, in either case, he must bind firmly around their bodies at or below the level of the armpits. The props must bind the hooker similarly. The hooker must not be supported so that he is not carrying any weight on either foot.

(c) The outside (loose-head) prop *must* either (i) bind his opposing (tight-head) prop with his left arm inside the right arm of his opponent, or (ii) place his left hand or forearm on his left thigh.
The tight-head prop *must* bind with his right arm outside the left upper arm of his opposing loose-head prop. He may grip the jersey of his opposing loose-head prop with his right hand but only to keep himself and the scrummage

steady and he must not exert a downward pull.

(d) All players in a scrummage, other than those in a front row, must bind with at least one arm and hand around the body of another player of the same team.

(e) No outside player other than a prop may hold an opponent with his outer arm.

Note: (6) It is permissible for the outside (loose head) prop to alter his binding with his left arm, within the provisions of Law 20 (6) (c), at any time during a scrummage.

PUTTING THE BALL INTO THE SCRUMMAGE

(7) The team not responsible for the stoppage of play shall put in the ball. In the event of doubt as to responsibility the ball shall be put in by the team which was moving forward prior to the stoppage or, if neither team was moving forward, by the attacking team.

Note: (7) A stoppage may be caused without any infringement by either team.

The words 'responsible for the stoppage of play' include legitimate actions by a team, such as falling on the ball, tackling, etc., which prevent the opposing team from continuing play.

(8) The ball shall be put in without delay as soon as the two front rows have closed together. A team must put in the ball when ordered to do so and on the side first chosen.

Notes: (8) In the interests of safety, the referee has authority to permit delay in putting in the ball if a player in the front row has not succeeded in getting his head down in the scrummage.

(9) A penalty kick should be awarded if the referee is satisfied that delay by the team in putting the ball in is deliberate and prejudices the other team.

(9) The player putting in the ball shall
  (a) stand one metre from the scrummage and midway between the two front rows;
  (b) hold the ball with both hands midway between the two front rows at a level midway between his knee and ankle;
  (c) from that position put in the ball
  ● without any delay or without feint or backward movement, i.e. with a single forward movement, and
  ● at a quick speed straight along the middle line so that it first touches the ground immediately beyond the width of the nearer prop's shoulders.

(10) Play in the scrummage begins when the ball leaves the hands of the player putting it in.

(11) If the ball is put in and it comes out at either end of the tunnel, it shall be put in again, unless a free kick or penalty kick has been awarded.

If the ball comes out otherwise than at either end of the tunnel and if a penalty kick has not been awarded play shall proceed.

Note: (10) Advantage applies as soon as the ball has been put into the scrummage and played.

RESTRICTIONS ON FRONT ROW PLAYERS

(12) All front row players must place their feet so as to allow a clear tunnel. A player must not prevent the ball from being put into the scrummage, or from touching the ground at the required place.

(13) No front row player may raise or advance a foot until the ball has touched the ground.

Note: (11) Until any foot is permitted to be raised or advanced, that foot must be kept in the normal position.

(14) When the ball has touched the ground, any foot of any player in either front row may be used in an attempt to gain possession of the ball subject to the following:

players in the front rows must not **at any time** during the scrummage:
  (a) raise both feet off the ground at the same time, or
  (b) wilfully adopt any position or wilfully take any action, by twisting or lowering the body or by pulling on an opponent's dress, which is likely to cause the scrummage to collapse, or

81

(c) wilfully kick the ball out of the tunnel in the direction from which it is put in.

Notes: (12) The prohibition against a player in the front row raising both feet off the ground at the same time or striking at the ball with both feet applies during the whole scrummage and not merely to the period while the ball is being put in.

(13) Referees must be strict in applying penalties for wilfully kicking out. Repeated kicking out **must** be treated as wilful.

(14) When the referee orders the ball to be put in again it **must** be put in by a player of the same team that was first entitled to do so.

(15) If the ball is about to pass straight through the tunnel and a far prop advances a foot so that the ball passes behind that foot, the ball must be put in again unless it has been lawfully played (i.e. touched) by a player in the front row.

RESTRICTIONS ON PLAYERS

(15) Any player who is not in either front row must not play the ball while it is in the tunnel.

(16) A player must not:
(a) return the ball into the scrummage, or
(b) handle the ball in the scrummage except in the act of obtaining a 'push-over' try or touch-down, or

(c) pick up the ball in the scrummage by hand or legs, or
(d) wilfully collapse the scrummage, or
(e) wilfully fall or kneel in the scrummage, or
(f) attempt to gain possession of the ball in the scrummage with any part of the body except the foot or lower leg.

Note: (16) Referees must be strict in penalising for the wilful collapsing of the scrummage as stated under Law 20 (16) (d) and Law 26 (3) (g).

(17) The player putting in the ball and his immediate opponent must not kick the ball while it is in the scrummage.

Note: (17) If a player repeatedly infringes, he **must** be dealt with under Law 26 (2).

Penalty: (a) **For an infringement of paragraphs (2), (5), (8), (9), (12), (13) and (15), a free kick at the place of infringement.**
(b) **For an infringement of paragraphs (1), (3), (4), (6), (14), (16) and (17), a penalty kick at the place of infringement.**

For Off-side at Scrummage see Law 24 B.

LAW 21 Ruck

A ruck, which can take place only in the field-of-play, is formed when the ball is on the ground and one or more players from each team are on their feet and in physical contact, closing around the ball between them.

Note: If the ball in a ruck is on or over the goal line the ruck is ended.

(1) A player joining a ruck must have his head and shoulders no lower than his
Ⓔ hips. He must bind with at least one arm around the body of a player of his team in the ruck.

Note: (1) The placing of a hand on another player is not binding. Binding involves the whole arm, from hand to shoulder.

(2) A player must not:
    (a) return the ball into the ruck, or
    (b) handle the ball in the ruck except in the act of securing a try or touch-down, or
    (c) pick up the ball in the ruck by hand or legs, or
    (d) wilfully collapse the ruck, or
    (e) jump on top of other players in the ruck, or
    (f) wilfully fall or kneel in the ruck, or
    (g) while lying on the ground interfere in any way with the ball in or

emerging from the ruck. He must do his best to roll away from it.

Penalty: Penalty kick at the place of infringement.

For Off-side at Ruck see Law 24 C.

LAW 22 Maul

A maul, which can take place only in the field-of-play, is formed by one or more players from each team on their feet and in physical contact closing round a player who is carrying the ball.

A maul ends when the ball is on the ground or the ball or a player carrying it emerges from the maul or when a scrummage is ordered.

Note: If the ball in a maul is on or over the goal line the maul is ended.

(1) A player joining a maul must have his head and shoulders no lower than his
Ⓔ hips. A player is not in physical contact unless he is caught in or bound to the maul and not merely alongside it.

(2) A player must not:
    (a) jump on top of players in a maul,
Ⓔ   or
    (b) wilfully collapse a maul, or

(c) attempt to drag another player out of the maul.

Penalty: Penalty kick at the place of infringement.

(3) When the ball in a maul becomes unplayable a scrummage shall be ordered and the team which was moving forward immediately prior to the stoppage shall put in the ball, or if neither team was moving forward, the attacking team shall put it in.

Notes: (1) Before whistling for a scrummage, the referee should allow a reasonable time for the ball to emerge from the maul, particularly if either team is moving forward. If in his opinion the ball will probably not emerge from the maul without delay, he should not allow prolonged wrestling for the ball but should order a scrummage.

(2) If any player in a maul goes to the ground, a scrummage is to be ordered.

Ⓔ

For Off-side at Maul see Law 24 C.

LAW 23 Touch and Line-out

A. Touch

(1) The ball is in touch
- when it is not being carried by a player and it touches a touch line or the ground or a person or object on or beyond it, or
- when it is being carried by a player and it or the player carrying it

touches a touch line or the ground beyond it.

(2) If the ball is not in touch a player who is in touch may kick the ball or propel it with his hand but not hold it.

Notes: (1) (a) If the ball pitches directly into touch from a kick-off and the opposing team elects to accept the kick, the line-out shall be formed
    (i) at the half-way line, or
    (ii) where the ball went into touch if that place be nearer to the kicker's goal line.

(b) If the ball pitches directly into touch from a drop-out and the opposing team elects to accept the kick, the line-out shall be formed where the ball went into touch.

(c) 'pitching directly into touch' means that the ball, having been kicked, first touches the touch line or the ground or a person or object on or beyond it and has not touched or been touched in flight by an opponent or the referee.

(2) On or beyond the touch line or touch-in-goal line refers to all areas except the playing area.

(3) It is **not** touch or touch-in-goal when a player with both feet in the playing area catches the ball, even though the ball before being caught has crossed the touch line or

touch-in-goal line. Such a player may deflect or tap the ball into the playing area provided it is not propelled forward. If a player jumps and catches the ball his feet must land in the playing area.

B. Line-Out

The line-of-touch is an imaginary line in the field-of-play at right angles to the touch line through the place where the ball is to be thrown in.

FORMATION OF LINE-OUT

(1) A line-out is formed by at least two players from each team lining up in single lines parallel to the line-of-touch in readiness for the ball to be thrown in between them. The team throwing in the ball shall determine the maximum number of players from either team who so line up. Such players are those 'in the line-out' unless excluded below.

Note: (4) Prior to the beginning of the line-out, any offence, including wilfully failing to form a line-out, or to line up at least two players, should be dealt with as misconduct under Law 26 (3) (h).

(2) Until the ball is thrown in each player in the line-out must stand at least one metre from the next player of his team in the line-out, and avoid physical contact with any other player.

Note: (5) The distance of 'at least one metre' means between players who are deemed to be facing the touch line and standing upright with their feet together. Players may adopt any stance and face in any direction.

(3) The line-out stretches from five metres from the touch line from which the ball is being thrown in to a position fifteen metres from that touch line.

(4) Any player of either team who is further than fifteen metres from the touch line when the line-out begins is **not** in the line-out.

(5) A clear space of 500 mm. must be left between the two lines of players.

Notes: (6) The distance of 500 mm. for the clear space is between the shoulders of the players when standing upright.

(7) If, at a formed line-out, the team throwing in the ball line up less than the normal number, their opponents must be given a reasonable opportunity to conform. Opposing players who are retiring for that purpose must do so directly and without delay to a line ten metres behind the line-of-touch. Loiterers must be penalised. Subject to this, when the line-out is ended

players so retiring may rejoin play, even if they have not reached the ten metres line.

THROWING IN THE BALL

(6) When the ball is in touch the place at which it must be thrown in is as follows:

- when the ball goes into touch from a penalty kick, free kick, or from a kick within twenty-two metres of the kicker's goal line, at the place where it touched or crossed the touch line, or

- when the ball pitches directly into touch after having been kicked otherwise than as stated above, opposite the place from which the ball was kicked or at the place where it touched or crossed the touch line if that place be nearer to the kicker's goal line, or

- on all other occasions when the ball is in touch, at the place where it touched or crossed the touch line.

In each intance the place is where the ball last crossed the touch line before being in touch.

(7) The ball must be thrown in at the line-out by an opponent of the player whom it last touched, or by whom it was carried, before being in touch. In the event of doubt as to which team should throw in the ball, the attacking team shall do so.

(8) The ball must be thrown in without delay and without feint.

(9) A **quick throw-in** from touch without waiting for the players to form a line-out is permissible provided the ball that went into touch is used, it has been handled only by the players and it is thrown in correctly.

Note: (10) At a quick throw-in the position of fifteen metres from touch requirement does not apply.

(10) The ball may be brought into play by a quick throw-in or at a formed line-out. In either event the player must throw in the ball

- at the place indicated, and

- so that it first touches the ground or touches or is touched by a player at least five metres from the touch line along the line-of-touch, and

- while throwing in the ball, he must not put any part of either foot in the field-of-play.

If any of the foregoing is infringed, the opposing team shall have the right, at its option, to throw in the ball or to take a scrummage.

If on the second occasion the ball is not thrown in correctly a scrummage shall be formed and the ball shall be put in by the team which threw it in on the first occasion.

Notes: (8) If a player wilfully prevents the ball from being thrown in five metres, a penalty kick should be awarded.

(9) If a player wilfully throws the ball in not straight a penalty kick should be awarded.

BEGINNING AND END OF LINE-OUT

(11) The line-out begins when the ball leaves the hands of the player throwing it in.

(12) The line-out ends when
- a ruck or maul is taking place and all feet of players in the ruck or maul have moved beyond the line-of-touch, or
- a player carrying the ball leaves the line-out, or
- the ball has been passed, knocked back or kicked from the line-out, or
- the ball is thrown beyond a position fifteen metres from the touch line, or
- the ball becomes unplayable.

Notes: (13) If a player participating in a line-out hands the ball to another player who is peeling off from the line-out, the line-out ends when the second player takes the ball.

(14) When the ball has been passed or knocked back from a line-out, the line-out is ended. Players in front of a player of their own team who receives the ball from the line-out may be off-side but they should only be penalised under Law 24 A if they play the ball or obstruct an opponent in any way.

(15) A ruck or maul has not moved from the line-of-touch unless all the feet of the players in the ruck or maul have moved beyond that line.

PEELING OFF

'Peeling off' occurs when a player (or players) moves from his position in the line-out for the purpose of catching the ball when it

has been passed or knocked back by another of his team in the line-out.

(13) When the ball is in touch players who approach the line-of-touch must **always** be presumed to do so for the purpose of forming a line-out. Except in a peeling off movement such players must not leave the line-of-touch, or the line-out when formed, until the line-out has ended. A player must not begin to peel off until the ball has left the hands of the player throwing it in.

Exception: At a quick throw-in, when a player may come to the line-of-touch and retire from that position without penalty.

(14) In a peeling off movement a player must move parallel and close to the line-out. He must keep moving until a ruck or maul is formed and he joins it or the line-out ends.

RESTRICTIONS ON PLAYERS IN LINE-OUT

(15) **Before** the ball has been thrown in and has touched the ground or has touched or been touched by a player, any player in the line-out must not
(a) be off-side, or
(b) push, charge, shoulder or bind with or in any way hold another

player of **either** team, or

(c) use any other player as a support to enable him to jump for the ball, or

(d) stand within five metres of the touch line or prevent the ball from being thrown five metres.

Notes: (11) Any movement of a player beyond a position fifteen metres from the touch line must be solely for the purpose of catching or jumping to catch the ball. The player may move in-field in an attempt to catch the ball only after it leaves the hand of the player throwing it in.

(12) A player acting as scrum-half may not stand or move beyond a position fifteen metres from the touch line before the ball has passed that position unless he moves to anticipate a long throw-in but he may so move only in accordance with the conditions in the preceding note (11).

(16) **After** the ball has touched the ground or touched or been touched by a player, any player in the line-out must not

(a) be off-side, or

(b) hold, push, shoulder or obstruct an opponent not holding the ball, or

(c) charge an opponent except in an attempt to tackle him or to play the ball.

(17) Except when jumping for the ball or peeling off, each player in the line-out must remain at least one metre

from the next player of his team until the ball has touched or has been touched by a player or has touched the ground.

(18) Except when jumping for the ball or peeling off, a clear space of 500 mm. must be left between the two lines of players until the ball has touched or has been touched by a player or has touched the ground.

Note: (16) The act of jumping for the ball can include a step if it is a simple movement in endeavouring to catch the ball.

(19) A player in the line-out may move into the space between the touch line and the five metres mark only when the ball has been thrown beyond him and, if he does so, he must not move towards his goal line before the line-out ends, except in a peeling off movement.

(20) Until the line-out ends, no player may move beyond a position fifteen metres from the touch line except as allowed when the ball is thrown beyond that position, in accordance with the Exception following Law 24 D (1) (d).

Note: (17) If the ball in a line-out becomes unplayable, otherwise than as a result of an infringement for which a penalty is prescribed, a scrummage should be ordered.

RESTRICTIONS ON PLAYERS NOT IN LINE-OUT

(21) Players of either team who are not in the line-out may not advance from behind the line-out and take the ball from the throw-in except only

- a player at a quick throw-in, or
- a player advancing at a long throw-in, or
- a player 'participating in the line-out' (as defined in Section D of Law 24) who may run into a gap in the line-out and take the ball provided he does not charge or obstruct any player in the line-out.

Penalty: (a) For an infringement of paragraphs (1), (2), (3), (4), (5), (8), (13), (17), (18) or (19) a free kick fifteen metres from the touch line along the line-of-touch.

(b) For an infringement of paragraphs (14), (15), (16) or (20), a penalty kick fifteen metres from the touch line along the line-of-touch.

(c) For an infringement of paragraph (21), a penalty kick on the offending team's off-side line (as defined in Law 24 D) opposite the place of infringement, but not less than fifteen metres from the touch line.

Place of scrummage: Any scrummage taken or ordered under this Law or as the result of any infringement in a line-out shall be formed fifteen metres from the touch line along the line-of-touch.

Note: (18) If a player repeatedly infringes, he **must** be dealt with under Law 26 (2).

For Off-side at Line-out see Law 24 D.

LAW 24 Off-side

Off-side means that a player is in a position in which he is out of the game and is liable to penalty.

In general play the player is in an off-side position because he is in front of the ball when it has been last played by another player of his team.

In play at scrummage, ruck, maul or line-out the player is off-side because he remains or advances in front of the line or place stated in, or otherwise infringes, the relevant sections of this Law.

A. Off-Side in General Play

(1) A player is in an off-side position if the ball has been
- kicked, or
- touched, or
- is being carried

by one of his team behind him.

(2) There is no penalty for being in an off-side position unless:
(a) the player plays the ball or obstructs an opponent, or
(b) he approaches or remains within ten metres of an opponent waiting to play the ball or the place where the ball pitches.

Where no opponent is waiting to play the ball but one arrives as the ball pitches, a player in an off-side position must not obstruct or interfere with him.

Exceptions: (i) When an off-side player cannot avoid being touched by the ball or by a player carrying it, he is 'accidentally off-side'. Play should be allowed to continue unless the

89

infringing team obtains an advantage, in which case a scrummage shall be formed at that place.

(ii) A player who receives an unintentional throw-forward is not off-side.

(iii) If, because of the speed of the game, an off-side player finds himself unavoidably within ten metres of an opponent waiting to play the ball or the place where the ball pitches, he shall not be penalised provided he retires without delay and without interfering with the opponent.

Penalty: Penalty kick at the place of infringement, or, at the option of the non-offending team, a scrummage at the place where the ball was last played by the offending team. If the latter place is In-goal, the scrummage shall be formed five metres from the goal line on a line through the place.

Notes: (1) A penalty for off-side should not be given at once if the non-offending team gains an advantage or if it appears likely to gain an advantage; but if the expected advantage is not gained, the penalty should in all cases be awarded even if it is necessary to bring play back for that purpose to the place of infringement.

(2) When a player knocks on and an off-side player of the same team next plays the ball, a penalty for off-side should not be awarded unless the off-side deprives the non-offending team of an advantage.

(3) A player can be off-side in his In-goal.

(4) If a player hands the ball to another player of his team in front of him, the second player is off-side. A scrummage for 'accidental off-side' should be awarded unless it is considered the player was wilfully off-side in which case a penalty kick should be awarded.

(5) The referee should whistle at once if an off-side player who cannot be placed on-side charges within ten metres of an opponent waiting to receive the ball. Delay may prove dangerous to the latter player.

Where there is no opponent **waiting** to play the ball but one arrives as the ball pitches, an off-side player who is near such an opponent must not obstruct or interfere with him in any way whatsoever before he is put on-side.

(6) If an attacking player kicks the ball which is mis-fielded by an opponent and the ball is then played by another attacking player in an off-side position within ten metres of the opponent, a penalty kick should be awarded.

(7) If an attacking player kicks the ball which is charged down by an opponent and another attacking player within ten metres of the opponent then plays the ball, play should be allowed to continue. The opponent was not 'waiting to play the ball' and the second attacking player is therefore on-side under Law 25 (2).

(8) Law 24 A (2) (b) also applies where the ball has struck a goal-post or crossbar. Off-side players must not approach or remain within ten metres of an opponent waiting to play the ball or the place where the ball pitches.

B. Off-Side at Scrummage

The term 'off-side line' means a line parallel to the goal lines through the hindmost foot of the player's team in the scrummage.

While a scrummage is forming or is taking place:

(1) A player is off-side if
   (a) he joins it from his opponents' side, or
   (b) he, not being in the scrummage nor the player of either team who puts the ball in the scrummage,
      ● fails to retire behind the off-side line or to his goal line whichever is the nearer, or
      ● places either foot in front of the off-side line while the ball is in the scrummage.

A player behind the ball may leave a scrummage provided he retires immediately behind the off-side line.

If he wishes to rejoin the scrummage, he must do so behind the ball.

He may not play the ball as it emerges between the feet of his front row if he is in front of the off-side line.

Exception: The restrictions on leaving the scrummage in front of the off-side line do not apply to a player taking part in 'wheeling' a scrummage provided he immediately plays the ball.

(2) A player is off-side if he, being the player of either team who puts the ball in the scrummage, remains, or places either foot, in front of the ball while it is in the scrummage, or

if he is the immediate opponent of the player putting in the ball, takes up position on the opposite side of the scrummage in front of the off-side line.

Penalty: Penalty kick at the place of infringement.

Notes: (9) Players must retire without delay to the scrummage off-side line when a scrummage is forming. Loiterers must be penalised.

(10) Any player of either team may at a particular scrummage be the player who puts in the ball or who takes up position as scrum-half when his opponent is putting in the ball; but such player is at that scrummage the only player of his team who has

the benefit of Law 24 B (2).

(11) If the scrummage has turned or wheeled through 180 degrees the true concept of the scrummage off-side line cannot be applied. Players not in the scrummage except the scrum-half shall, however, not proceed beyond the nearer scrummage off-side line. In these circumstances, any player whose position in the scrummage is such that his feet represent the 'hindmost' feet in that particular scrummage, if he has continued binding throughout the turn or wheel, is permitted to detach himself from the scrummage provided he **immediately** picks up the ball which is at his feet. On his so doing the scrummage is at an end.

C. Off-side at Ruck or Maul

The term 'off-side line' means a line parallel to the goal-lines through the hindmost foot of the player's team in the ruck or maul.

(1) RUCK OR MAUL OTHERWISE THAN AT LINE-OUT

While a ruck or maul is taking place (including a ruck or maul which continues after a line-out has ended) a player is off-side if he:

(a) joins it from his opponents' side, or

(b) joins it in front of the ball, or

(c) does not join the ruck or maul but fails to retire behind the off-side line **without delay** or

(d) unbinds from the ruck or leaves the maul and does not **immediately** either rejoin it behind the ball or retire behind the off-side line, or

(e) advances beyond the off-side line with either foot and does not join the ruck or maul.

Penalty: Penalty kick at the place of infringement.

(2) RUCK OR MAUL AT LINE-OUT

The term 'participating in the line-out' has the same meaning as in Section D of this Law. A player participating in the line-out is not obliged to join or remain in the ruck or maul and if he is not in the ruck or maul he continues to participate in the line-out until it has ended.

While a line-out is in progress and a ruck or maul takes place, a player is off-side if he:

(a) joins the ruck or maul from his opponents' side, or

(b) joins it in front of the ball, or

(c) being a player who is participating in the line-out and is not in the ruck or maul, does not retire to and remain at the off-side line defined in this Section, or

Penalty: Penalty kick fifteen metres from the touch-line along the line-of-touch.

(d) being a player who is not participating in the line-out, remains or advances with either foot in front of the off-side line defined in Section D of this Law.

Penalty: Penalty kick on the offending team's off-side line opposite the place of infringement, but not less than fifteen metres from the touch line.

Note: (12) When the line-out has ended but the ruck or maul is still taking place, a player is off-side if he infringes Section (1) of these Laws.

D. Off-Side at Line-out

The term 'participating in the line-out' refers exclusively to the following players:
- *those players who are in the line-out, and*
- *the player who throws in the ball, and*
- *his immediate opponent who may have the option of throwing in the ball, and*
- *one other player of either team who takes up position to receive the ball if it is passed or knocked back from the line-out.*

All other players are **not** *participating in the line-out.*

The term 'off-side line' means a line ten metres behind the line-of-touch and parallel to the goal lines or, if the goal line be nearer than ten metres to the line-of-touch, the 'off-side line' is the goal line.

OFF-SIDE WHILE PARTICIPATING IN LINE-OUT

(1) A participating player is off-side if:

(a) **before** the ball has touched a player or the ground he wilfully remains or advances with either foot in front of the line-of-touch, unless he advances solely in the act of jumping for the ball, or

(b) **after** the ball has touched a player or the ground, if he is not carrying the ball, he advances with either foot in front of the ball, unless he is lawfully tackling or attempting to tackle an opponent who is participating in the line-out. Such tackle or attempt to tackle must, however, start from his side of the ball, or

(c) in a peeling off movement he fails to keep moving close to the line-out until a ruck or maul is formed and he joins it or the line-out ends, or

(d) before the line-out ends he moves beyond a position fifteen metres from the touch line.

Exception: Players of the team throwing in the ball may move beyond a position fifteen metres from the touch line for a long throw-in to them. They may do so only when the ball leaves the hands of the player throwing it in and if they do so their opponents participating in the line-out may follow them. If players so move and the ball is not thrown to or beyond them they must be penalised for off-side.

Penalty: Penalty kick fifteen metres from the touch line along the line-of-touch.

Notes: (15) Players who advance beyond the off-side line or who move beyond a position fifteen metres from the touch line in the expectation of a long throw-in must be penalised if, for any reason, the ball is not thrown beyond that position.

(16) A player jumping unsuccessfully for the ball who crosses the line-of-touch should be given an opportunity to retire before being penalised.

(17) The referee should be strict in dealing with those players who, while not disputing possession of the ball in the line-out, advance to an off-side position whether intentionally or not.

(2) The player throwing in the ball and his immediate opponent must:
   (a) remain within five metres of the touch line, or
   (b) retire to the off-side line, or
   (c) join the line-out after the ball has been thrown in five metres, or
   (d) move into position to receive the ball if it is passed or knocked back from the line-out provided no other player is occupying that position at that line-out.

Note: (14) If a player other than the wing-threequarter throws in the ball from touch, the wing-threequarter must retire to the off-side line, or join the line-out.

OFF-SIDE WHILE NOT PARTICIPATING IN LINE-OUT

(3) A player who is not participating is off-side if before the line-out has ended he advances or remains with either foot in front of the off-side line.

Exception: Players of the team throwing in the ball who are not participating in the line-out may advance for a long throw-in to them beyond the line-out. They may do so only when the ball leaves the hands of the player throwing in the ball and, if they do, their opponents may advance to meet them. If players so advance for a long throw-in to them and the ball is not thrown to them they must be penalised for off-side.

Note: (13) If a player not participating in the line-out is off-side, the referee should not whistle immediately if the opposing team is likely to gain an advantage. He should apply the advantage law in all such cases.

PLAYERS RETURNING TO 'ON-SIDE' POSITION

(4) A player is not obliged, before throwing in the ball, to wait until players of his team have returned to or behind the line-out but such players are off-side unless they return to an on-side position **without delay.**

Penalty: Penalty kick on the offending team's off-side line (as defined in Section D of this Law) opposite the place of infringement but not less than fifteen metres from the touch line.

Note: (18) Scrummage, Ruck, Maul and Line-out – where these Laws state a line which determines the off-side position such line stretches continuously from touch line to touch line.

LAW 25 On-side

On-side means that a player is in the Game and not liable to penalty for off-side.

PLAYER MADE ON-SIDE BY ACTION OF HIS TEAM

(1) Any player who is off-side in general play, **including** an off-side player who is within ten metres of an opponent waiting to play the ball or the place where the ball pitches and is retiring as required, becomes on-side as a result of any of the following actions of his team:

- when the off-side player has retired behind the player of his team who last kicked, touched or carried the ball, or
- when one of his team carrying the ball has run in front of him, or
- when one of his team has run in front of him after coming from the place or from behind the place where the ball was kicked.

  In order to put the off-side player on-side, this other player must be in the playing area, but he is not debarred from following up in touch or touch-in-goal.

Note: (1) An off-side player who is within ten metres of an opponent waiting to play the ball or the place where the ball pitches must retire and continue to do so up to ten metres until he is put on-side. If he does not do so, he must be penalised.

PLAYER MADE ON-SIDE BY ACTION OF OPPOS-
ING TEAM

(2) Any player who is off-side in general play, **except** an off-side player within ten metres of an opponent waiting to play the ball or the place where the ball pitches, becomes on-side as a result of any of the following actions:

- when an opponent carrying the ball has run five metres, or
- when an opponent kicks or passes the ball, or
- when an opponent **intentionally** touches the ball and does not catch or gather it.

An off-side player within ten metres of an opponent waiting to play the ball or the place where the ball pitches **cannot** be put on-side by **any** action of his opponents.

Any **other** off-side player in general play is **always** put on-side when an opponent plays the ball.

PLAYER RETIRING AT SCRUMMAGE, RUCK, MAUL OR LINE-OUT

(3) A player who is in an off-side position when a scrummage, ruck, maul or line-out is forming or taking place and is retiring as required by Law 24 (Off-side) becomes on-side:

- when an opponent carrying the ball has run five metres, or
- when an opponent has kicked the ball.

An off-side player in this situation is **not** put on-side when an opponent passes the ball.

Notes: (2) The referee should be careful to ensure that no benefit under Law 25 (2) is gained by loiterers who wilfully remain in an off-side position and thereby prevent opponents from running with, kicking, passing or otherwise playing the ball.

(3) When a team has gained quick possession from a scrummage, ruck, maul or line-out and starts a passing movement, opponents who are retiring must not be allowed to interfere with the movement unless the conditions of Law 25 (3) exist. Referees should be strict in applying this.

LAW 26 Foul Play

Foul Play is any action by a player which is contrary to the letter and spirit of the Game and includes obstruction, unfair play, misconduct, dangerous play, unsporting behaviour, retaliation and repeated infringements.

OBSTRUCTION

(1) It is illegal for any player:

(a) who is running for the ball to charge or push an opponent also running for the ball, except shoulder to shoulder,

(b) who is in an off-side position wilfully to run or stand in front of another player of his team who is carrying the ball, thereby preventing an opponent from reaching the latter player,

(c) who is carrying the ball after it has come out of a scrummage, ruck, maul or line-out, to attempt to

force his way through the players of his team in front of him,

(d) who is an outside player in a scrummage or ruck to prevent an opponent from advancing round the scrummage or ruck.

Penalty: Penalty kick at the place of infringement. A penalty try may be awarded.

Notes: (1) There are no circumstances in which a player carrying the ball can be penalised for obstruction.

(2) The referee should note that:
   (a) The intention of this Law as regards the penalties to be imposed for serious forms of obstruction must be applied.
   (b) If a player is guilty of charging or obstructing or holding an opponent who is not carrying the ball or any other form of foul play, before any other action is taken the player

must at once be cautioned or sent off. If he offends a second time, the referee has no alternative to sending him off. If the offence prevents a try which **probably** would otherwise have been scored, a penalty try must be awarded.

(c) The intention of the International Board is that if the referee has any doubt as to the balance of probability, he should give the benefit of the doubt in favour of the non-offending team and award the penalty try.

UNFAIR PLAY, REPEATED INFRINGEMENTS

(2) It is illegal for any player:
   (a) deliberately to play unfairly or wilfully infringe any Law of the Game,
   (b) wilfully to waste time,
   (c) wilfully to knock or throw the ball from the playing area into touch, touch-in-goal or over the dead-ball line.
   (d) to infringe repeatedly any Law of the Game.

Penalty: Penalty kick at the place of infringement. A penalty try may be awarded. For offences under 2 (c) occurring in In-goal, Law 14 penalty (e) applies.

For offences under 2 (d) a player may be cautioned and, if he repeats the offence, must be ordered off.

MISCONDUCT, DANGEROUS PLAY

(3) It is illegal for any player:

(a) to strike an opponent,

(b) wilfully to hack or kick an opponent or to trip him with the foot or to trample on an opponent lying on the ground,

(c) to tackle early, or late or dangerously, including the action known as 'a stiff arm tackle',

(d) who is not running for the ball wilfully to charge or obstruct an opponent who has just kicked the ball,

(e) to hold, push, charge, obstruct or grasp an opponent not holding the ball except in a scrummage, ruck or maul,

(*Except in a scrummage or ruck the dragging away of a player lying close to the ball is permitted. Otherwise pulling any part of the clothing of an opponent is holding.*)

(f) in the front row of a scrummage to form down some distance from the opponents and rush against them,

(g) wilfully to cause a scrummage, ruck or maul to collapse,

(h) while the ball is out of play to molest, obstruct or in any way interfere with an opponent or be guilty of any form of misconduct,

(i) to commit any misconduct on the playing area which is prejudicial to the spirit of good sportsmanship.

Penalty: A player guilty of misconduct or dangerous play shall either be ordered off or else cautioned that he will be sent off if he repeats the offence. For a similar offence after caution, the player must be sent off.

In addition to a caution or ordering off a penalty try or a penalty kick shall be awarded as follows:

(i) **If the offence prevents a try which would otherwise *probably* have been scored, a penalty try shall be awarded.**

(ii) **The place for a penalty kick shall be:**

(a) **For offences other than under paragraphs (d) and (h), at the place of infringement.**

(b) **For an infringement of (d) the non-offending team shall have the option of taking the kick at the place of infringement or where the ball alights, and if the ball alights**

● ***in touch,* the mark is fifteen metres from the touch line on a line parallel to the** goal lines through the place where it went into touch, or

- *within fifteen metres from the touch line*, it is fifteen metres from the touch line on a line parallel to the goal lines through the place where it alighted, or

- *in In-goal, touch-in-goal, or over or on the dead-ball line*, it is five metres from the goal line on a line parallel to the touch line through the place where it crossed the goal line or fifteen metres from the touch line whichever is the greater. When the offence takes place in touch the 'place of infringement' in the optional penalty award is fifteen metres from the touch line opposite to where the offence took place. If the offence takes place in touch-in-goal Law 14 penalty (d) applies.

(c) For an offence under (h), at any place where the ball would next have been brought into play if the offence had not occurred, or, if that place is on the touch line, fifteen metres from that place, on a line parallel to the goal lines.

(iii) *For an offence in In-goal*, a penalty kick is to be awarded *only* for offences under Law 14, *Penalty* (d) and Law 26 (3) (h).

(iv) For an offence under Law 26 (3) (h), the penalty kick is to be taken at whichever is the place where play would re-start, that is

- at the twenty-two metre line (at any point the non-offending team may select), or

- at the centre of the half-way line, or

- if a scrummage five metres from the goal line would otherwise have been awarded, at that place or fifteen metres from the touch line on a line five metres from and parallel to the goal line, whichever is the greater.

(v) For an offence which occurs outside the playing area while the ball is still in play and which is not otherwise covered in the foregoing, the penalty kick shall be awarded in the playing area fifteen metres from the touch line and opposite to where the offence took place.

(vi) **For an offence reported by a touch judge under Law 6 B (6) a penalty kick may be awarded where the offence occurred or at the place where play would restart.**

Notes: (3) 'Playing the man without the ball' and all forms of dangerous tackling including early, late and stiff arm 'tackling' or tackling or attempting to tackle a player around the neck or head **must** be punished severely. Players who wilfully resort to this type of foul play must be sent off the field. A penalty try must be awarded if the late tackle prevents a probable try.

(4) It is for the referee to decide what constitutes a dangerous tackle, having regard to the circumstances, e.g., the apparent intentions of the tackler, or the nature of the tackle, or the defenceless position of the player being tackled or knocked over, which may be the cause of serious injury.

(5) It is for the referee to determine in the circumstances of the particular case whether the following actions constitute dangerous play:

(a) If a player charges or knocks down an opponent carrying the ball without any attempt to grasp him (as in a tackle);

(b) If a player taps or pulls the foot or feet of another player who is jumping in a line-out; but this is prima facie dangerous play.

(6) A player shall not 'take the law into his own hands' nor wilfully do anything that is dangerous to an opponent even if the latter is infringing the Laws.

(7) If a player is obstructed after kicking the ball and the ball strikes a goal post, the optional penalty should be awarded where the ball alights after bouncing off the post.

(8) If a penalty kick has been awarded and, before the kick has been taken, the offending team infringes Law 26 (3) (h), the referee should

(a) caution or send off the player guilty of misconduct and

(b) in addition advance the mark for the penalty kick ten metres, this to cover both the original infringement and the misconduct.

(9) If a penalty kick is awarded to a team and before the kick is taken, a player of that team

infringes Law 26 (3) (h) the referee should

(a) caution or send off the player guilty of misconduct and

(b) declare the penalty kick void and

(c) award a penalty kick against the team last guilty of misconduct.

(10) The referee should note that:

(a) Repeated infringement is a question of fact and not a question of whether the offender intended to infringe.

(b) If the same player has to be penalised repeatedly he should be dealt with under Law 26 (2) (d).

(c) Foul play must not be condoned.

(d) Repeated infringements arise mainly in connection with Scrummages, Off-side and Line-outs. If a player has been penalised for infringing one of these Laws several times in the same match, he should be cautioned and, if he repeats the offence, sent off.

(e) It is a question for the referee whether or not a series of the same offences by different players of a team amounts to repeated infringement. If he considers that it does, he should give a general warning to that team and, if the offence is repeated, he must send the offending player off the field.

(f) In deciding the number of offences which should constitute 'repeated infringement' the referee should always apply a strict standard in representative and senior matches. On the third occasion a caution must be given.

In the case of junior or minor matches where ignorance of the Laws and lack of skill may account for many infringements, a less strict standard may be applied.

(11) The International Board and the Unions in membership with it will fully support referees in the strict and uniform enforcement of the Law as to repeated infringements.

PLAYER ORDERED OFF

A player who is ordered off shall take no further part in the match. When a player is ordered off, the referee shall, as soon as possible after the match, send to the Union or other disciplinary body having jurisdiction over the match a report naming the player and describing the circumstances which necessitated the ordering off. Such report shall be considered by the Union or other disciplinary body having jurisdiction over the match who shall take such action and inflict such punishment as they see fit.

LAW 27 Penalty Kick

A penalty kick is a kick awarded to the non-offending team as stated in the Laws.

It may be taken by any player of the non-offending team and by any form of kick provided that the kicker, if holding the ball, must propel it out of his hands or, if the ball is on the ground, he must propel it a visible distance from the mark. He may keep his hand on the ball while kicking it.

(1) The non-offending team has the option of taking a scrummage at the mark and shall put in the ball.

(2) When a penalty kick is taken the following shall apply:

(a) The kick must be taken without undue delay.

(b) The kick must be taken at or behind the mark on a line through the mark and the kicker may place the ball for a place kick. If the place prescribed by the Laws for the award of a penalty kick is within five metres of the opponents' goal line, the mark for the penalty kick or a scrummage taken instead of it shall be five metres from the goal line on a line through that place.

(c) The kicker may kick the ball in any direction and he may play the ball again, without any restriction, except that if he has indicated to the referee that he intends to attempt a kick at goal or has taken any action indicating such intention he must not kick the ball in any other way. Any indication of intention is irrevocable.

(d) The **kicker's team** except the placer for a place kick must be behind the ball until it has been kicked.

(e) The **opposing team** must run without delay (and continue to do so while the kick is being taken and while the ball is being played by the kicker's team) to or behind a line parallel to the goal lines and ten metres from the mark, or to their own goal line if nearer to the mark. They must there remain motionless with their hands by their sides until the kick has been taken.

Retiring players will not be penalised if their failure to retire ten metres is due to the rapidity with which the kick has been taken, but they may not stop retiring and enter the game until an opponent carrying the ball has run five metres.

(f) The **opposing team** must not prevent the kick or interfere with the kicker in any way. This applies to actions such as wilfully carrying, throwing or kicking the ball away out of reach of the kicker.

Penalty:
● **For an infringement by the _kicker's team_ - a scrummage at the mark.**

● **For an infringement by the _opposing team_ - a penalty kick ten metres in front of the mark or five metres from the goal line whichever is the nearer on a line through the mark. Any player of the non-offending team may take the kick.**

Notes:
(1) The kick must be taken with the ball which was in play unless the referee decides that the ball is defective.

(2) The note (9) under Law 13 applies also in the case of a penalty kick.

(3) A player taking a penalty kick may not bounce the ball on his knee. The kick must be made with the foot or lower leg. If a player fails to kick the ball, a scrummage should be ordered.

(4) In addition to the general provision regarding waste of time, the kicker is bound to

kick without delay, under penalty.

The instructions in the second paragraph of note (1) on Law 13 apply also in the case of a penalty kick.

Even without a caution, if the delay is clearly a breach of Law the kick should be disallowed and a scrummage ordered.

(5) The referee must always make up time lost by any delay in taking the kick, as provided for in note (2) under Law 5.

(6) If the kicker appears to be about to take a kick at goal, the referee may ask him to state his intention.

(7) If the kicker is taking a kick at goal, all players of the opposing team must remain passive from the time the kicker commences his run until the kick has been taken.

(8) When a penalty kick is taken in In-goal, a penalty try may be awarded if a defending player by foul play prevents an opponent from first grounding the ball.

(9) If, from a penalty kick taken in In-goal, the ball travels into touch-in-goal or over the dead-ball line, a five metres scrummage should be ordered, the attacking team to put in the ball.

(10) If the kicker takes a drop kick and a goal results, the goal stands even though the kicker has not indicated to the referee an intention to kick at goal.

(11) If, notwithstanding a prior infringement by the opposing team, a goal is kicked, the goal should be awarded instead of a further penalty kick.

(12) The referee should not award a further penalty if he is satisfied that the reason for such further penalty has been deliberately contrived by the kicker's team, but should allow play to continue.

LAW 28 Free Kick

A free kick is a kick awarded for a fair-catch or to the non-offending team as stated in the Laws.

A goal shall not be scored from a free kick by the kicker unless the ball has been first played by another player.

For an infringement it may be taken by any player of the non-offending team.

It may be taken by any form of kick provided that the kicker, if holding the ball, must propel it out of his hands or, if the ball is on the ground, he must propel it a visible distance from the mark. He may keep his hand on the ball while kicking it.

(1) The team awarded a free kick has the option of taking a scrummage at the mark and shall put in the ball.

(2) When a kick is taken, it must be taken without undue delay.

(3) The kick must be taken at or behind the mark on a line through the mark and the kicker may place the ball for a place kick.

(4) If the place prescribed by the Laws for the award of a free kick is within five metres of the opponents' goal line, the mark for the free kick, or the scrummage taken instead of it, shall be five metres from the goal line on a line through that place.

(5) The kicker may kick the ball in any direction and he may play the ball again without restriction.

(6) The **kicker's team,** except a placer for a place kick, must be behind the ball until it has been kicked.

(7) The **opposing team** must not wilfully resort to any action which may delay the taking of a free kick. This includes actions such as wilfully carrying, throwing, or kicking the ball away out of reach of the kicker.

(8) The **opposing team** must retire without delay to or behind a line parallel to the goal lines and ten metres from the mark or to their own goal line if nearer to the mark. Having so retired, players of the opposing team may charge with a view to preventing the kick, as soon as the kicker begins his run or offers to kick.

   Retiring players will not be penalised if their failure to retire ten metres is due to the rapidity with which the kick has been taken, but they may not stop retiring and enter the game until an opponent carrying the ball has run five metres.

(9) If having charged fairly, players of the opposing team prevent the kick from being taken it is void.

(10) Neither the kicker nor the placer shall wilfully do anything which may lead the opposing team to charge prematurely. If either does so, the charge shall not be disallowed.

Penalty:
● **For an infringement by the *kicker's team* or for a void kick a scrummage at the mark and the *opposing team* shall put in the ball.**

   If the mark is In-goal, the scrummage shall be awarded five metres from the goal line on a line through the mark.

● **For an infringement by the *opposing team* - a penalty kick ten metres in front of the mark or five metres from the goal line whichever is nearer on a line through the mark. Any player of the non-offending team may take the kick.**

   If the mark is In-goal, a drop-out shall be awarded.

Notes:
(1) The kick must be taken with the ball which was in play unless the referee decides that the ball is defective.

(2) A player taking a free kick may not bounce the ball on

his knee. The kick must be made with the foot or lower leg. If a player fails to kick the ball, a scrummage should be ordered.

(3) The kicker may not feint to kick and then draw back. Once he makes any movement to kick, the opponents may charge.

(4) In addition to the general provision regarding waste of time, the kicker is bound to kick without delay, under penalty.

(5) The referee shall see that the opposing players do not gradually creep up and that they have both feet behind the ten metres line, otherwise he shall award a penalty kick in accordance with the penalty provisions of Law 28.

(6) If the kick is taken from behind the goal line, the ball is in play if an opponent legitimately plays it before it crosses the goal line, and a try may be scored.

(7) When a free kick is taken in In-goal, a penalty try may be awarded if a defending player, by foul play, prevents an opponent from first grounding the ball.

(8) If from a free kick taken in In-goal, the ball travels into touch-in-goal or over the dead-ball line, a five metres scrummage should be ordered, the attacking team to put in the ball.

(9) If opponents lawfully charge

down a free kick in the playing area, play should be allowed to continue.

(10) If a free kick has been awarded in the field-of-play and the player retires to his In-goal to take the kick and his opponents having lawfully charged prevent the kick from being taken, a scrummage shall be awarded five metres from the goal line on a line through the mark.

(11) If a free kick has been awarded in In-goal and the opponents having lawfully charged prevent the kick from being taken, a scrummage shall be awarded five metres from the goal line on a line through the mark.

(12) The referee should not substitute a penalty kick for a free kick if he is satisfied that the reason for such a penalty has been deliberately contrived by the kicker's team, but should allow play to continue.